BOTH SIDES
OF
THE BORDER

BOTH SIDES
OF
THE BORDER

TERRY BUTCHER

with

Andy Cairns

ARTHUR BARKER
An imprint of George Weidenfeld and Nicolson Limited
London

To Rita, Christopher and Edward

Published in Great Britain by
George Weidenfeld & Nicolson Limited
91 Clapham High Street
London SW4 7TA

ISBN 0 213 16950 9

Printed in Great Britain by
Butler & Tanner Ltd, Frome and London

Contents

Acknowledgements

My thanks go to Andy Cairns for his perseverance through thick and thin. Thanks also to Donna McPherson for suggesting the title and to Sylvia Cairns (Andy's mum) for her help typing the manuscript.

I would also like to thank everyone who has helped me during my career, including my parents for their support and co-operation during the early years. And a special word of thanks to Mike Regis: without him none of this would have been possible.

PICTURE ACKNOWLEDGEMENTS

The photographs in this book are reproduced by kind permission of the following:
All-Sport (1, 31)
Terry Butcher (2, 3, 4, 16, 17)
Mark Leech (19)
Alan MacGregor Ewing (22)
Rangers News (18, 20, 23, 24, 25, 26)
Sportapic (21)
Bob Thomas (5, 6, 7, 9, 10, 11, 12, 13, 14, 15, 27, 28, 29, 30)
Weidenfeld and Nicolson (8)

1

I Belong to Glasgow

When I joined Glasgow Rangers there were people in England who thought I must be crazy. I admit that when Graeme Souness, the new Rangers manager, first approached me I never really thought I would end up at Ibrox. Graeme had taken over in April and his move had caused quite a surprise. He was at the peak of his playing career with the Italian club Sampdoria and was still an important figure in the Scotland World Cup squad due to leave for Mexico that summer.

Every time I played against Graeme Souness I wanted to kick him. He always ran the show against us, whether he was playing for Scotland or his old club Liverpool, and his arrogance and the way he strutted around the pitch as though he owned it made players want to bring him down a peg or two. So when I first spoke to him I was astounded to find that he was very polite, courteous and charming. He was also very persuasive. 'I'm trying to build the best team in Britain,' he said, 'I want you to be the captain.'

At the time I wasn't sure what was happening or where I was going. I was hoping to join Manchester United and was disappointed when they didn't make a bid. For a while I thought I was going to join Chelsea, and I was waiting to hear whether Tottenham would make an offer which was acceptable to Ipswich. The idea of an Englishman skippering one of the most famous clubs in Scotland had an appeal of its own but seemed an unlikely eventuality. But Souness wouldn't give up and persuaded me to go to Glasgow and have a look.

Once I saw Ibrox for myself I knew what Graeme meant when he talked about Rangers being a big club. There is a history and tradition about Rangers that is quite unique. The old, mahogany-panelled entrance hall leads up to one of the most magnificent trophy rooms I have ever seen – packed with cups and pennants, including one from Ipswich when we played there in 1981. But for a club with so many reminders of the past there was a feeling of a great future as well. They had spent £10 million on three new stands, and the stadium is one of the most modern in Europe with 35,000 seats.

There was a feeling about the place that they were on the verge of something big. Above all, there was a passion among the fans which made me realize how important Rangers FC is to so many people. The club is a major Scottish institution. I had been astonished at the stature of the club and the size of the support, and the only doubt I had about signing was whether the fans would take to me. But from my arrival they were superb. Before I signed people came up to me in the street and said how much they hoped I would join Rangers.

For my first game, a pre-season friendly against Bayern Munich, more than 36,000 turned up. That was nearly double Ipswich's average home gate and higher than the average attendance at Anfield when Liverpool won the League and Cup double the previous season. The fans were marvellous, and although I didn't understand very many of the chants I could at least recognize my own name! There is a long walk along the tunnel from the dressing room to the pitch at Ibrox and, as you approach the end, you hear the noise mount to a crescendo as you walk out. It's a fantastic feeling.

Too many people in England fail to appreciate how big the game is in Scotland. The standard of football is a lot higher than many people think and the top five or six teams in Scotland would hold their own in the top half of the English First Division. Support for the top clubs, like Rangers and Celtic, matches anything south of the border, and in my first season with Rangers demand for tickets was so great that all our away games were sold out weeks in advance. When tickets for home games went on sale enormous queues would form right round the ground.

You could sense that the fans were hungry for success. For

years Rangers had dominated Scottish football, but recently they had been challenged and often outshone by Celtic, Aberdeen and Dundee United. Within three months we gave everyone connected with Ibrox something to cheer about when we won the Skol Cup. Beating Celtic in the final at Hampden Park made it even sweeter.

I have played football all over the world, but there is nothing that compares with the atmosphere at an Old Firm game. The noise is louder than anything I have ever known, and while in other games with a good atmosphere there is generally a lull in the noise once the game is underway in Glasgow the fans keep on at the same level for all ninety minutes. A goal from Ian Durrant and a penalty from Davie Cooper six minutes from time were enough to give us the cup.

I was the proudest man in Britain. Like the Rangers fans I had waited a long time to win something, collecting just one medal in nearly ten years of first team football. Being presented with the cup was a special moment for me, the latest highpoint in a career which has seen its share of ups and downs.

When I was first approached to write this book I didn't think that I had much to say, but as I look back over my time in football there have been incidents which have made me chuckle and others which have made me cry.

It's a career which has seen me enjoy the good times with Ipswich Town as we rose to become one of the best teams in Europe, winning the UEFA Cup in 1981 with our own exciting style of football. I also experienced the bad times as the club slipped down the table, eventually being relegated five years later.

It's a career which has given me great pleasure, but almost cost me my life after a horrifying injury during an FA Cup game at Luton. And it's a career which has taken me around the globe for club and country – to two World Cup Finals and now to Glasgow as captain of one of the most famous teams in the world. I hope you enjoy this country boy's tale.

2

Starting Out

When I was sixteen if anyone had told me that I would eventually play for Ipswich, England and Rangers I would have thought they were mad. Although I loved football I didn't think I was anywhere near good enough to make it as a professional and, at the age when other lads joined clubs as apprentices, I stayed at school to take my 'O' and 'A' levels. I was all set to go to polytechnic and study to become a quantity surveyor before there was any real suggestion that I might become a footballer.

I was born in Singapore on 28 December 1958. The record books show that on that day Rangers were top of the Scottish First Division, despite having lost 2–1 to Third Lanark the day before. In England, the reigning league champions, Wolves, were three points clear at the top of the First Division. Ipswich, who had spent most of their brief league career in Division Three South, were finding their feet in the higher echelons of the Second Division.

My father, who was stationed in Singapore with the navy, celebrated the birth of his first child in style. He spent the night going from bar to bar, getting exceedingly drunk and buying drinks for anyone he met. He also found a trumpet and was heard wandering the streets in the early hours in a loud and disorderly fashion. Somehow he escaped arrest and we stayed in Singapore for several months before moving back to Petersfield in Hampshire for a while and then returning to Lowestoft in Suffolk where both my parents had grown up.

My mother, Valerie, says that I was an active child and, by the time I was nine months old, I was running about kicking a ball. Over the next few years I ruined the lawn in our back garden and was in constant trouble for smashing the fence after using it for shooting practice. Anyone who has seen my shooting in recent years will probably wonder how I managed to hit the fence at all!

When I was old enough I used to go to a local park, called the Fen, and play football with my friends for hours on end. Occasionally, we would join in a game with a few grown ups. My father, a renowned left-back in his day, or so he says, always fancied himself as a useful player, especially against the younger lads.

I was football crazy and we would have games in the backstreets on our way home from school, using our blazers as goal-posts. I was always wearing out my shoes kicking a football, tennis ball or even stones, and was out playing football every day except Sunday when my sister Vanda and I had to go to Sunday school.

The best place to play in Lowestoft was the local beach, miles and miles of glorious golden sand. Each morning we would read the tide charts and, if it was low tide, we would be straight down to the beach to play football. My friend, David Baldry, and I would be the first there and the last home.

When it got dark we would move the pitch and play floodlit games under the bright lights from the pier. My parents had a beach hut in Lowestoft and we spent our summer holidays there playing every sport imaginable. Although the games exhausted my father, he at least had the consolation that his lawn and fence were having a rest. The constant practice on the beach helped me develop a love of most sports.

However, my first competitive game was a complete disaster. Although I was two years younger than the rest of the team, I was picked for Fen Park primary school first eleven. We played the old 2–3–5 formation and I was left-back, under strict instructions to stay in that position and not to move. It was an inauspicious start to my career and we lost 7–1. We had one more game, another defeat, and the team was disbanded, much to the relief of our goalkeeper.

On Saturday afternoons my father used to take me to watch Lowestoft Town play in the Eastern Counties League. But I was more interested in finding a ball and playing behind the goal.

I was nearly nine years old when I saw my first professional game. My father had supported Ipswich since he was a boy and took me to see them play Aston Villa at home. It was during the 1967–8 season: the year Ipswich won the Second Division. We stood in the North Stand and I couldn't get over the noise of the crowd; more than 17,000 people who all seemed to be singing and shouting at once. I remember Ipswich were 1–0 down at half-time and came back to win 2–1 with goals from Colin Harper and Eddie Spearritt.

The team had some great names: Ken Hancock in goal, Tommy Carroll and Billy Houghton at full-back and Billy Baxter, the captain, at centre-half. Colin Viljoen and Danny Hegan were in midfield and Ray Crawford was centre-forward. And the number six shirt was worn by a rising star called Mick Mills. I became a confirmed Ipswich fan and to see my heroes in action was always a big thrill.

Ipswich won promotion that season and I became a regular for the big First Division games at Portman Road over the next few years. Bill McGarry had left and was replaced as manager by Bobby Robson. He built a new team, and people like Mick Lambert, Trevor Whymark and Allan Hunter became my new heroes. But there was one player I admired above the rest and that was Kevin Beattie.

We saw some great games, including a memorable 4–1 win against Manchester United who had Best, Law and Charlton in their team. That was a sweet victory for me because my sister Vanda was a United fan and I was able to remind her about that result for the rest of the season.

We were a very close family and my parents were always willing to take us out for the day along the Suffolk coast with a few of our friends. I was quite shy, and if I wasn't playing football I would come home and watch television particularly my favourite programmes like 'The Monkees', 'Voyage To the Bottom of the Sea' and 'Scooby Do'. My parents and my grandfather encouraged me to read and I grew to love books. We spent hours leafing through the adventures of Thomas the

Tank Engine and I enjoy reading the same books to my own children.

I enjoyed school and was quite bright when I was younger so I was put forward to take my eleven-plus a year early. I passed and went to Lowestoft Grammar School when I was ten. When I arrived, I found to my horror that you had to play rugby in the autumn term and could only play football in the spring. And, if you did not play rugby then you were not allowed to play football.

The PE teacher, Dan Maddock, although a strict disciplinarian, gave us plenty of encouragement. I began to enjoy rugby and settled in as a fly-half, mainly because I was the only one who could kick the ball a long way. Rugby is a hard game and I am sure that it toughened me up, physically and mentally, which came in useful in later years for football. After seeing some of my tackles, there are people who still think I cannot distinguish between the two sports! I could not have been too bad as I captained the First XV for two years, and although I have not played for a while I still enjoy watching a good game of rugby particularly when England win the Calcutta Cup.

In the summer I enjoyed cricket and athletics and was quite successful in the sprints and high hurdles, although these days I am much better at long distances. But football was still my main love.

In those days I played in goal for the school team. I had to borrow the gloves and jersey from my friend, David Baldry, but my main contribution was to shout and scream at the top of my voice. It drove Mr Maddock mad. He said I was the loudest goalkeeper he had ever heard and in one game he threatened to send me off unless I quietened down. I think I only stayed on the pitch that day because nobody else fancied going in goal.

When I was fifteen I joined Fen Park FC, a Sunday morning men's team. My mother was not very pleased because it meant that I would miss church, but she accepted that I would rather be playing football. Soon I was playing four games every weekend. I would play for school on Saturday mornings, Ashlea in the Anglian Combination League on Saturday afternoons, Fen Park on Sunday mornings and if there was another game in the afternoon, I would play in that. If not, I would go over to the park for a kick around with the lads.

I played in some weird and wonderful places in those days and travelled all over Norfolk and Suffolk for away games. I remember playing at places like Southrepps and Wells in north Norfolk. Facilities were basic and we would often have to change in a draughty barn or even in the car. Showers were rare and often after a game we would have to wash with a grubby sponge and a bucket of cold water before a long drive home still half covered in mud.

Some of the pitches looked as though they had been ploughed rather than mown and the grounds were often exposed to the icy east winds which blew fresh from the coast. It was football at the grass roots – a million miles from Wembley Stadium – and I loved every minute of it.

I hadn't found a settled position on the field. I played in goal one week against Carrow and pulled off some great saves before one of their players nut-megged me for the equalizer. I didn't live that down for several months. Other weeks I played left-back or centre-half, and one week I even played in midfield and scored four – it must have been a miracle!

For the school I had moved outfield and was picked to play for Lowestoft boys and then Suffolk schools. I was even invited for a trial with England schoolboys. The invitation said boys should pay particular attention to a 'smart appearance', so I had a haircut, cleaned my school blazer and set off to join the other hopefuls at Bisham Abbey.

The trial was one of the biggest disappointments of my life. The selectors turned me down because they said I could not head a ball. The rejection hurt. I was never a confident boy and I found it hard to take when people said: 'Sorry son, you are not good enough.' After that I always tried to avoid putting myself in positions where people could make similar decisions about me.

When there was a suggestion that West Ham might offer me a trial I told everyone I was not interested. I wanted to be a footballer but I did not think I was good enough and I certainly did not want to be rejected again.

Our family did not know anyone in professional football and, although some youngsters are pushed into the game by their parents, it never crossed my mother and father's minds that their son could make a career in the game.

The only game my dad pushed me into was playing for the Blundeston Prison Officer's team. He was an officer there and occasionally ran the line for them, calling me in if they were short. I have never played with such a great bunch of people. Prison officers have a difficult job but stick together through thick and thin, especially in their social club after a game. Since then I have always enjoyed a few pints and a chat after a game at any level of football.

We had a great run in the Prison cup and, with my father running the line in his pork-pie hat and keeping a sharp eye for opposing forwards who strayed off-side, we had a good defensive record.

There was one bizarre game at Lothingland psychiatric hospital in Suffolk. The match was constantly interrupted by patients wandering across the pitch and stopping and chatting to the players. The game would be held up for several minutes while a couple of nurses ran on to take the patients back to the sidelines. Then another patient would casually wander on, and we would have another wait before more nurses arrived to persuade them to leave.

When I was in the sixth form at school people kept asking what I would do when I left. I didn't have a clue. I had passed seven 'O' levels and was happy to plod through life, play football with my mates and listen to groups like Queen and Deep Purple on my stereo. I thought briefly about the police force, but my dad wasn't keen. He wanted me to be a lawyer which I didn't fancy at all.

My mother worked in a careers office, but even with such expert advice so close to hand I couldn't decide on my future. I had met some quantity surveyors who were friendly and seemed to get out and about a bit and, as I was quite good at maths and there was nothing else on the horizon, I settled for that. I applied for a course at Trent Polytechnic and was all set to go there after my 'A' levels. The thought of being a footballer never entered my head.

I had spent a few evenings training at Ipswich towards the end of the season but nothing had come of it. I was with boys who were two or three years younger than me. I was twice their size, felt very self-conscious and didn't do too well.

I had been recommended by Mike Regis, who was the secretary of the Lowestoft branch of the Ipswich Town supporters club. He kept on and on until they invited me and, once the evening sessions finished, he kept up his pressure and bombarded the club with letters insisting that they offer me a trial.

His persistance finally paid off. I had finished my exams when I received a letter inviting me for a three-week trial at Portman Road in August. I often wonder what would have happened if Mike hadn't made such a nuisance of himself on my behalf and I shall always be indebted to him.

In the meantime I received an unexpected offer of a trial at Norwich, having been recommended by the manager of a local Sunday side. But I had mixed feelings. I was an Ipswich fan through and through and, however much the idea of being a footballer appealed to me, the thought of playing for our closest rivals filled me with horror.

People talk about the rivalry between Liverpool and Everton on Merseyside and Celtic and Rangers in Glasgow but in East Anglia feelings run just as high between the Norwich and Ipswich fans.

The trial was terrible. I didn't know anyone. All the other lads were on trial as well. We played a game but I didn't know where to play or who to pass to and couldn't wait to get away. I still think trials like that are unfair. It's also impossible for a club to make a sound judgement about a player after watching him in one game with twenty-one strangers. There's no time to assess a boy's temperament, personality or character, all of which are as important as skill if he is to make it to the top.

It was a different story at Ipswich. The lads who were on trial spent up to a month at the club so the coaching staff got to know us. I was shaking with nerves when I first arrived at Portman Road. About four or five of us were on trial and we stood around looking awkward on one side of the changing room while reserves and apprentices who had already been taken on laughed and joked on the other. I changed quickly and quietly and was too scared to speak to anyone.

Although I was shy I enjoyed going in each day. The club made us feel part of things and I was making a bit of money from my travelling expenses. They had also taken one look at my boots and given me a new pair. But the biggest thrill was being so close to the players I had idolized from the terraces just a few months earlier.

I played for the youth team in some pre-season friendlies and heard a few encouraging comments from the coaches but I didn't know how well I had done or what they thought of me. Then one day I went in and there was a message that Bobby Robson wanted to see me. All sorts of thoughts rushed through my head and my legs were like jelly by the time I got to his office.

Bobby greeted me with a smile and said the club wanted to sign me, not as an apprentice but as a professional. The contract was for one year initially and the wages would be £50 a week, with a £2 bonus for a win and a £1 bonus for a draw. I couldn't believe my ears. It was a fortune for a seventeen-year-old and only £10 a week less than my dad was earning. I would have signed for nothing, but agreed to talk things over with my parents.

My mother was against it. She had seen enough boys in the careers office who had set their hearts on becoming footballers and been discarded after a year or so. 'Go to college and get some qualifications,' she said. But my father was all for it. He was an Ipswich fan and was as excited as I was. As a concession to my mother we wrote to Trent Polytechnic and asked them to keep my place open for a year, in case things didn't work out.

I went straight into the youth team for Ipswich's first league game of the 1976–77 season, away to Arsenal. Russell Osman and I were the twin centre-halves and we clicked immediately. It was the start of a long and successful partnership. Our team also included Alan Brazil, while Steve Gatting, the brother of the England cricket captain Mike, was in the Arsenal team. After going a goal down we came back to win 2–1 and could have had more.

That afternoon we arrived back in Ipswich in time to see the first team beat Tottenham 3–1, and my day was complete when I was told that I was to be thirteenth man for the reserves the following Tuesday. They were away at Queen's Park Rangers and it was a big boost for a new boy. There was no chance of me playing unless one of the team was taken ill at the last minute, but I was delighted to go along and help with the kit.

The reserve team coach was Bobby Ferguson who had a reputation as a gruff Geordie. After doing my jobs I took my seat next to him on the bench and settled down to enjoy the game. After a few minutes we went one up then Robin Turner made a mistake and Ferguson exploded. He leapt off the bench like a jack-in-the-box and started shouting and swearing. Among other names, he called Robin a 'ruptured crab'. This struck me as funny and I laughed. What a mistake!

Fergie span round looking even angrier. He pointed at me and screamed: 'Laugh lad. You laugh at me. I'll make you cry before you're finished.'

The other lads knew what he was like and shrugged it off, but I was used to having a laugh and joke during a game and hadn't been prepared for such an outburst. It was my introduction to Bobby Ferguson.

I soon found that life as a professional was not going to be easy. Charlie Woods, the youth team coach, took me to one side and said: 'Son, your passing is bad, your control is bad and your heading is bad. For a footballer you haven't got much of a start.' He told me to practise my skills by knocking a ball against the wall under the stand, which I did every morning before training. And then he told me that my co-ordination was hopeless and gave me a skipping rope. 'Skip properly and it will improve your footwork,' he said.

The training was obviously much harder than anything I had been used to and with an eighty mile round trip from Lowestoft to Ipswich each day I was becoming exhausted. On the way home I would fall asleep on the train before it could pull out of Ipswich station.

We decided I should move into digs in Ipswich. I had a marvellous landlady, Mrs Seggars, who went out of her way to make me feel at home. John Stirk, a young reserve team player, was already there and we became firm friends and are still in touch today.

It also meant that I could spend more time with the other

lads. In the past I had felt a bit of an outsider. When they went off to the café after training I would have to rush off home to Lowestoft. Now I could join in, and after lunch several of us would go back to the ground for extra training and ball work.

It was physically demanding for a seventeen-year-old. We would have to be at the ground just after nine in the morning and do our jobs before training. I managed to avoid looking after the boots and was put in charge of the drying room and sorting out the kits for the first team and the reserves.

Then we would have a strenuous training session and after lunch we'd come back for extra practice. I'd arrive home at Mrs Seggars' house and fall asleep in front of the fire every afternoon. Sometimes I would just about have enough energy to eat my tea and go to bed in the evening. I think the coaches hoped that if they made us tired we wouldn't have the energy to get up to any mischief in the local hostelries.

We had a very good team and won the South East Counties League by six points. Several of that side made it as professionals with Russell Osman, Alan Brazil and myself eventually breaking into the Ipswich first team. Alan had a fantastic season and scored around forty goals. He was picked for the Scotland youth team while Russell played for England youth and was voted Ipswich's 'Young Player of the Year'. Noel Parkinson, Ian Phillips and Dave Hubbick went on to play for Colchester and Steve Gardiner played for a team in Sweden.

Most of our games were on Saturday mornings and, for away games at places like Portsmouth, we would have to be up and ready to leave Ipswich by five o'clock. If we were at home we would have to watch the reserves or the first team in the afternoon and then clean up the changing rooms. With my size eleven feet I was a popular choice to replace divots on the pitch.

At the end of the season, Bobby Robson included me in the first team squad for testimonial games at Chelmsford and Cambridge. Allan Hunter and Kevin Beattie were away for the Home Internationals, so Russell and Dale Roberts took over at the centre of the defence with me as cover.

I came on in both games, and against Chelmsford I had the chance to mark Jimmy Greaves, one of the greatest goalscorers of all time who was still turning out for the non-league side.

The closest I got to him was when he called the referee over to stop the game after I received a cut above my eye. It needed several stitches and I had to go off, even though I had only been on the pitch a few minutes.

I must have done enough to impress Bobby Robson, however, as I was included in the squad for the end of season tour to Canada and Hawaii. I could hardly believe it. A year ago I had been taking my 'A' levels, now I was off around the world playing football.

The first team had finished third that season and were ready to enjoy the tour. I was a naïve country boy and it was all new to me, the travelling, the hotels and the night-clubs. I was wide-eyed and open-mouthed, especially when we ended up in a strip bar in Toronto. It was late at night and we'd been up to no good all evening. I was revelling in this new found lifestyle when I noticed two hulks walking towards me, both looking extremely unpleasant.

It was then that I realized the rest of the lads had gone and left me on my own. I had read about sleazy clubs like this and as these bruisers closed in I felt sure that I was in for a good hiding, when suddenly a lift door flew open and Robin Turner rushed out and pulled me back in, just in time.

It wasn't the last scary moment of the trip. In Vancouver I was woken up one night by my room-mate Pat Sharkey. Pat came in, very drunk and homesick, brandishing an empty wine bottle. I grabbed my wallet and my camera and ran down the corridor to seek refuge in Russell's room until Pat calmed down. Eventually the drink and tiredness got the better of him and he went to sleep, so I was able to creep back to my bed. Pat could be volatile when sober, but when he was in that kind of mood it was definitely not the time for reasonable conversation.

I came back to Lowestoft quite satisfied with life. I had been offered a new contract with a £15 a week pay rise, I'd been on tour with the first team and I'd come back with a glorious sun tan which I couldn't wait to show off on Lowestoft beach. Unfortunately it was cloudy every day. But apart from the weather, everything was looking rosy. Little did I know how tough life was going to be over the next few months.

3

The Going Gets Tough

I can hear the insults now. 'Butcher, you pansy! Butcher, you're like an old woman! Butcher, you're pathetic!' Not chants from opposition fans, this was Bobby Ferguson, the Ipswich reserve team coach. He made my life so miserable that I came close to giving up football.

My first season had been a great success. The youth team had won the league and the club seemed pleased with my progress. But I soon learned that in football whenever you are on an up, there's always a down waiting just around the corner.

At eighteen I was too old for the youth team and the next step should have been the reserves. But combination football is a much harder game and I found it difficult to establish a regular place. Allan Hunter and Kevin Beattie were in the first team and Russell Osman and Dale Roberts were the regular centre-backs in the reserves. I was the fifth choice centre-half and only played if one of the others was injured or suspended. Most weeks I was fourteenth or fifteenth man so I didn't even get on as substitute.

I was still learning the difference between playing football as a professional and playing for fun. My father was a great believer in the traditions of schoolboy football and had brought me up to play as a sportsman. If I knocked someone over, I would help them up and make sure that they weren't hurt. When I did this at a professional club people laughed at me.

The coaches said I had to be aggressive. But it wasn't in my nature and in practice games I was scared to tackle the first team players in case I hurt them. People like Allan Hunter and Kevin Beattie were my heroes and it didn't seem right for me to go in hard against them.

My troubles with Fergie started during a reserve team game against Reading. I scored an own goal, lobbing the ball over our goalkeeper's head from thirty yards. We lost 3–2 and Fergie went bananas.

The criticism continued every time I played. Everyone could hear as his comments echoed around the virtually empty grounds. The more he shouted, the more my confidence drained away and the worse I played.

Among other things Bobby Ferguson called me a camel and nicknamed me Nat Jackley after the clumsy music-hall comedian, saying my legs were all over the place. Things reached rock bottom after a home game against Plymouth. We were always expected to beat such teams and, with ten minutes to go, were leading 2–0. Then I made two mistakes and they levelled the scores.

Afterwards Fergie stormed into the changing room, threw his coat on the floor and went berserk. He shouted at me until he was blue in the face. He said I couldn't tackle and that I would never make the big time. I remember sitting there with my ears burning and my eyes watering, too upset to answer back. He went on for an hour after the game.

My father was outside and heard everything. When I came out he could see that I was upset and wanted to go back and punch Ferguson. I managed to persuade him that if I left it to my dad to fight my battles it would only reinforce Fergie's opinion that I was too soft.

I hoped things would improve but they didn't. Ferguson picked on me all through the following week in training. It was relentless.

I thought: 'This is terrible. I can't go on like this.' I was a quiet, easy going, Suffolk lad. Being on the receiving end of all this bullying was turning me into a nervous wreck.

I went home to Lowestoft and told my parents that I was going to quit. My mother was all for it. 'That's right son,' she said, 'You come home to us. We'll show that horrible man he can't treat you like that.' But my father, who had wanted to thump Fergie a few days earlier, told me not to be stupid. 'Don't give in to his bullying,' he said. 'Go back and show them what you can do.'

My father was right, and I went back determined to succeed. Fergie has since told me that he was trying to make me tough and outgoing and bring me out of myself. He said: 'When I give people stick, it's because I want them to become better players. When I don't give you stick you should start to worry.'

Looking back I suppose he did me a lot of good and made me into the player I am today. Although I did not appreciate it at the time, I owe him a great deal. He made me say: 'Right, I'll show him' and I started to progress. I have seen other youngsters put through a similar routine and it does show whether they have any character to fight back. But I still think there must be better ways of bringing on youngsters than by humiliating them in front of their friends.

Kevin Beattie was injured for much of the 1977–8 season so Russell took his place in the first team. That meant that I had a lengthy run in the reserves and, with my new determination and Fergie off my back, my form improved.

We went on to finish third in the Football Combination that year and I had several good games. Towards the end of the season, Fergie kept recommending me for the first team and, during training one week in April, Bobby Robson called me to one side and said that I would be playing against Everton on the Saturday.

The lads had beaten West Brom at Highbury the week before in the FA Cup semi-final so everyone was looking forward to Wembley. But our League form had been disappointing and we were still fighting relegation. Hunter, Beattie and Roberts were all injured, so I was in and playing alongside my best pal Russell. I couldn't believe it, especially as my chances had looked so slim earlier in the season.

I would be marking Bob Latchford, who was the First Division's leading scorer and needed three more goals to win £10,000 from a national newspaper for being the first player to reach thirty that season. The lads were winding me up about that all week!

We spent the night in a hotel outside Liverpool and I roomed with David Geddis who did his best to keep me calm. As the coach took us to the ground I was astonished at the thousands of people on their way to the game. Everton were in second place in the league and were obviously looking for both points.

I was as white as a ghost when we got off the coach. There were hundreds of fans waiting for us and they crowded round Mick Mills and the other internationals for autographs and ignored me completely. My parents had driven up from Lowestoft and forced their way through the mob to wish me luck. I was so nervous that I couldn't speak. I opened my mouth a few times but nothing came out.

The changing rooms at Goodison Park are enormous and I sat in the corner shaking in my boots anxiously waiting for the game to start. Bobby Robson just told me to do my best and wished me luck.

The game flew by. We lost 1–0, Bob Latchford scoring from a penalty after Russell was judged to have fouled Martin Dobson. I tired a bit after an hour but played quite well and got a pat on the back from Mr Robson. My parents drove back to Lowestoft in time to see the game on Match of the Day that evening. The team flew back to Ipswich and Russell and I, suitably refreshed after a few beers, watched the programme from the comfort of the First Floor Club, a night-spot in the town centre.

The following Tuesday I was in the team again. We flew back to Merseyside, this time to play Liverpool at Anfield. I was to mark Kenny Dalglish. Playing in front of the Kop was something I had dreamed of as a boy on Lowestoft beach and I had to pinch myself to make sure that I was really there.

Trevor Whymark gave us the lead, before Dalglish and Graeme Souness scored for Liverpool. But we were playing well, and, with ten minutes to go, Mick Lambert scored again to give us a 2–2 draw and a valuable point. The Liverpool team had appealed for off-side but a certain midfield player had been slow to come out leaving Lambert on-side and unmarked. The culprit was one Graeme Souness.

Early on David Geddis had elbowed Tommy Smith in the face. PING! The whole crowd heard it and held its breath to see how Tommy, one of football's hard men, would react. You could see his expression change from disbelief that someone had whacked him to rage and one of the most threatening looks I have ever seen. The referee arrived to stop any trouble, but Tommy looked so angry I expected steam to pour out of his ears. Ten minutes later David Geddis was lying in a crumpled heap. Tommy Smith had gained his revenge.

I had soon found out that first team football was not going to be easy. I had marked two of the best forwards in the country, but had done reasonably well and received some good reports in the newspapers. One article quoted Bill Shankly saying that if he was still the Liverpool manager he 'would offer so much money for Butcher they wouldn't be able to turn it down'. It was very flattering but I knew I had a long way to go. And at Ipswich there was no chance of anyone getting ideas above their station.

To emphasize the point I was back in the reserves two days later and travelling down by train to play at Bristol City in front of a few hundred people. It seemed a long way from a packed Anfield.

Allan Hunter recovered from injury and returned to the first team, so I stayed in the reserves until the last game of the season when I made my home début against Wolves.

The lads had beaten Arsenal three days earlier to win the FA Cup for the first time in the club's history. Hunter and Beattie, who had been patched up for the final, were both receiving treatment so Russell and I were called in to play together at the back.

It was a special moment for me. I had stood on the terraces at Portman Road and dreamed of playing for Ipswich. Now I was making my first team home début and with 26,000 fans and a great atmosphere inside the ground, the stage was set for what should have been a memorable match.

It all went wrong. We were terrible, and after twenty minutes Wolves had taken a 2–0 lead. I played badly and some of the other lads looked as though they were still drunk from the weekend celebrations. We improved slightly in the second half and John Wark pulled one goal back, but it wasn't enough.

The crowd were obviously disappointed and started heckling. A group near my mother started picking on me. Obviously they didn't know that her son was wearing the number six shirt, but after she couldn't bear to hear her boy criticized any more she rounded on them and told them to shut up and give the lad a chance. Good old mum!

While the rest of the lads celebrated the end of the season around the Ipswich night-spots I felt very depressed. People had told me how great it would be to play in front of your own supporters. But we had lost and I felt responsible for the defeat. The season was over so there was no chance for me to redeem myself.

Still there was plenty to look forward to. I was included in the squad for the end of season tour to Majorca and Norway and I had tasted the high life of first team football. Ipswich had stayed in the First Division and won the FA Cup and there was a feeling around the club that we were on the verge of something really big.

4

The Tough Get Going

Winning the FA Cup in 1978 put Ipswich Town on the football map. People began to realize that we could play a bit in Suffolk and over the next few years we became the talk of football. We grew to be a force in Europe, won the UEFA Cup in 1981 and were voted European Team of the Year. For a small club with limited resources it was a considerable achievement.

I had made just two first team appearances before the FA Cup final against Arsenal and wasn't included in the Wembley squad. There were fitness doubts about Allan Hunter and Kevin Beattie, but in the end both were able to play. Mick Lambert was substitute and Russell Osman, who had played in the first team for most of the season, was thirteenth man.

Ever since I was a boy I had dreamed about seeing Ipswich play at Wembley, so I was just thrilled to be there. I went with a party from the club that included reserve team players, office staff, cleaning ladies and players' wives. We were determined to enjoy our big day out and seeing the twin towers and the thousands of Ipswich fans draped in blue and white brought a lump to my throat.

The bookmakers had made Arsenal firm favourites. They had finished fifth in the League and had players like Pat Jennings, Liam Brady, Alan Hudson and Malcolm Macdonald who were all potential match winners. But Ipswich were superb on the day. We controlled the game and Paul Mariner hit the bar and John Wark twice hit the post. I remember thinking we would never score when, with just over ten minutes to go, Roger Osborne beat Pat Jennings with a left foot shot. I went bonkers.

Ipswich had never won the FA Cup before and that night they celebrated in style. The club paid for everything. They put us up at the Royal Garden Hotel in Kensington and provided a sparkling reception with all the food and drink you could want. Russell and I even tried a couple of complimentary cigars in honour of our success. We puffed away for ages trying to light them and were blue in the face before someone explained about clipping the ends.

The next day more than 100,000 people lined the streets of Ipswich to welcome home the team and the Cup as they paraded in an open top bus. It was the team's day, and the reserves like me stood around awkwardly in the background. Bobby Robson introduced all the players to the crowd from the Town Hall balcony. There were huge cheers for players like Mick Mills and Kevin Beattie, but when he introduced me there was no reaction at all!

Now the club had tasted success all the players were hungry for more. We had seen the lift it gave the town and the supporters. The papers were predicting future glories for Ipswich and there was a feeling that the cup-winning side would go on to greater things.

Bobby Robson had his own plan for success, however, and in September he paid £150,000 for Arnold Muhren from the Dutch club, FC Twente. Tottenham had already shocked the football world a month earlier by signing the Argentine players Ossie Ardiles and Ricky Villa who had both featured in their country's successful World Cup campaign that summer. Now Ipswich had surprised everybody by signing a Dutch international midfield player who was unheard of in this country.

More than 28,000 fans turned up to see Arnold make his début at home to Liverpool. But it was Graeme Souness who stole the show, chipping Paul Cooper from thirty yards for one spectacular goal. We were awful and lost 3–0. People went home wondering what all the fuss was about and there were some inside the club who thought Arnold might prove to be an expensive mistake. To be fair, he must have been wondering if he had done the right thing as well. In his first few games he rarely saw the ball unless it was flying backwards and forwards above his head. He was used to a game where the ball was played through midfield. The Ipswich style at the time was based on banging the ball forward as early as possible, often by-passing the midfield.

Most people had expected the cup-winning side to stay together, but there were a few more changes to come. If Arnold's arrival had caused a few raised eyebrows, the departure of Brian Talbot to Arsenal for £450,000 caused an uproar in Suffolk. Brian was an Ipswich lad, an action man on the pitch with tremendous stamina. He was only twenty-four, had already won five full England caps and was a firm favourite with the crowd who saw him as a key player for the future.

Within weeks of his departure, Bobby Robson had paid £200,000 for Frans Thijssen, another unknown midfield player from FC Twente. The ban on overseas players had only been relaxed that summer and most clubs considered it too big a gamble to risk signing continentals who they felt would not adapt to the rigours of the First Division. It was a marvellous piece of foresight by Bobby Robson to sign both Arnold and Frans, and over the next few years, along with John Wark, they were to form one of the most effective midfield partnerships in the country.

Our early form in the 1978–79 season was disappointing and by Christmas we were stuck firmly in the bottom half of the table. I had again missed a chance to play at Wembley, this time in the curtain raiser for the new season, the Charity Shield, against the League champions, Nottingham Forest. Both Allan Hunter and Kevin Beattie were injured, but on the morning of the game I was lying in bed in hospital after fracturing a cheekbone in an accidental clash of heads with George Burley during a pre-season friendly in Belgium. John Wark was moved to the back four but our makeshift side lost 5–0.

My one game in the first half of that season was, ironically, away to Forest. We played quite well, but lost 1–0 to a Martin O'Neill goal which took a wicked deflection off my boot totally deceiving Paul Cooper. I had to wait until just before Christmas for my next chance when I was called in as a last minute replacement for Kevin Beattie. He had strained a groin during a five-a-side game in training. It was typical Kevin Beattie. The pitch was wet and greasy and everyone else wore studs except Kevin, who wore rubber soles. Inevitably he stretched and slipped and went down holding his leg. Bobby Robson was furious to say the least.

The next day we were away at Tottenham and again lost 1–0 to another deflected shot. It was my fifth first team game and I still hadn't been on a winning side. As I lay in the bath I started to think that I could be a jinx. But that elusive first victory came the following week at home to Bolton, although I nearly missed the game after injuring myself in training the day before.

We had been doing some sprints and I still had my spikes on. Instead of changing them when we went on to do some heading practice I kept them on ... and spiked myself on my right calf. I was carried off with blood pouring from the cut. It needed three stitches and Bobby Robson went berserk at my stupidity. It was touch and go whether I would play the next day but I was desperate and determined to make it.

Luckily I did quite well and had a hand in the first goal. I was up for a corner and the ball landed at my feet in front of goal. I think most people expected me to have a go, but I could see Paul Mariner in a better position and laid the ball square for him to score. I felt better after that and we went on to win 3–0

That win sparked a revival and we started climbing the table eventually finishing sixth after losing only twice in our next twenty-three games. Russell, myself and Alan Brazil, who had all played together in the same youth team, were now establishing ourselves in the first team. Alan, who was nick-named Pele for obvious reasons, scored nine goals in fourteen games. We were all thrown in at the deep end, and I found myself marking some of the best forwards in the country, players like Kenny Dalglish and Trevor Francis, who had just become Britain's first £1 million pound footballer when he joined Nottingham Forest.

I also had my first taste of European football. We were drawn against the famous Spanish side, Barcelona in the quarter finals of the Cup Winners' Cup. In the first leg at Portman Road we laid siege to their goal but could only score twice, Eric Gates getting them both. But one moment of slack defence had let them in to pull one back for a crucial away goal.

Some of the more experienced players tried to warn me what to expect in the return leg in Spain, but when we arrived in the Nou Camp it was louder and more hostile than I had imagined. We had trained at the stadium on the night before the game and hundreds of Barcelona fans came along to heckle and catcall at us. For the game there were 100,000 Spaniards expecting to see us get beaten. There was so much noise you had to shout to make yourself heard by people just a few feet away.

The game saw us under pressure for long periods as they kept pressing forward. Eventually Migueli scored a scrappy goal, his weak header bouncing three times on its way into the net through a crowd of players. We came close to pulling it off when Kevin Beattie came on as substitute and worried them with two late efforts, but we couldn't score and went out on away goals. Despite our exit, it was an enjoyable baptism into European football. I had marked the Austrian international Hans Krankl and the experience was to stand me in good stead for future ties abroad.

My career had really taken off in the last few months and I was called in to the England Under-21 squad after only eight first team appearances for Ipswich. Russell was already in the squad and I was called in to replace Sunderland's injured defender, Shaun Elliott. Stan Cummins was also in the squad, and the photographers had a good time taking pictures of us together. Stan was a little under five feet four inches tall while I was over a foot taller. We played Wales at Swansea and won 1-0. It was a terrible night and rained throughout the game. I didn't get on, but it was quite an experience just to be involved with the England set up.

I was learning all the time. Reserve team football had been fast and furious with ambitious youngsters rushing around anxious to impress. In the First Division you seemed to have more time, but teams didn't give away possession so easily which meant defenders had to mark tightly at all times. I was also less naïve and learning to look after myself. When I first broke into the team I would go up for high balls like an innocent and was being back-headed and elbowed. I picked up a painful collection of cuts and bruises from pros who never missed a chance to flex their muscles. Allan Hunter taught me how to protect myself and jump with one arm in front to keep daylight between my face and my opponent's head – a trick which has become even more invaluable in Scotland!

The next season Bobby Ferguson was promoted to first team coach. He replaced Cyril Lea who had left to join Stoke City. None of us were surprised when Cyril left as we had sensed an atmosphere between him and Bobby Robson during a pre-season tour of Holland. Cyril was one of the most honest men in football and had helped build the cup-winning side. He believed in getting the ball forward as quickly as possible and his advice was always 'If in doubt kick it out.' Fergie had been the reserve team coach, and most of us who had played for him knew he was a hard taskmaster and a shrewd tactician.

That run at the end of the 1978–79 season had set us in good heart and there was an air of expectancy about the club, especially as the two Dutchmen had settled in so well. Arnold had overcome his disastrous début and was now a firm favour-ite with the supporters who had voted him Ipswich Player of the Year.

Arnold was undoubtedly a great player with some marvellous skills. He was a good athlete and could run all day and, although he wasn't that tall, he was good in the air. But his main strength was his left foot; he could do anything with it. He was happy using the inside or the outside of the foot and could bend a ball whichever way he wanted. He used to moan about us knocking long balls forward, especially when they missed the target. He said: 'Give the ball to us [him and Frans Thijssen] and let us take it forward.' The pair of them showed what they could do with accurate passing and their continental style rubbed off on us. They became the level we aspired to.

The two Dutchmen improved my game enormously. In training we all worked harder to iron out our weaknesses and I would have competitions with Arnold to see who could score the most goals with their right foot. I had been stronger with my left foot since a childhood accident when I dropped a pot of scalding tea and badly burned my right leg. I've still got the scar and for months I had to wear a polythene covering to protect the wound. It didn't stop me playing football, but I soon grew used to kicking with my left foot and got out of the habit of using my right.

Frans Thijssen soon showed that he was another world class player. He could pass a ball well, but dribbling was his main strength. Once he got the ball you could never win it off him. He had superb balance and could twist and turn and wriggle his way out of the tightest situations. He would tease defenders by showing them the ball and when they lunged in for a tackle they would find that he had gone and taken the ball with him. He seemed to have an extension to his leg which would stretch out and hook the ball back, then he would be off leaving a trail of defenders in his wake. He caught us with this trick so often in training that the lads soon named him Captain Hook.

Although they were inevitably thought of as a pair, the Dutch lads were completely different off the pitch as well as having distinctive styles on it. Arnold was an introvert who kept himself to himself, didn't drink much and rarely came out with the lads unless his wife was in Holland. Frans wanted to do all the things that Arnold didn't. He was always ready to go for a few beers and loved a good laugh and a night with the boys.

All footballers like a good old moan and Arnold was no exception. He would complain about the length of training, the weather, the food and, if things were going really badly, he would start swearing to himself in Dutch and taught us all a few choice expressions. But he was always a popular figure. On a pre-season tour of Holland he insisted on showing us a short-cut to the ground. As he was a local it seemed a good idea, but as kick-off time approached it became quite obvious we were lost. We made it on time eventually, but the journey took two hours longer than it would have done on the main roads. Arnold didn't live that down for a long time and was never invited to the front of the coach again.

Every pre-season we would tour Holland and with Arnold and Frans to guide us round the Amsterdam night-spots we invariably found the right place to quench our thirst. Dutch beer is much stronger than its English counterpart and we would regularly roll back way after curfew, sneaking in the back entrance or climbing up the drainpipe to avoid the manager's spies. But the following morning at the daily team meeting the boss was always able to single out the night-clubbers. In four pre-season tours I was fined every year.

Gradually a new system had started to evolve. Up front Eric Gates was tucked in behind Paul Mariner and Alan Brazil. Most of our play went through midfield where Frans and Arnold flanked John Wark. But Eric was the key. The rest of the team and our pattern of play was moulded around him. Our game was based on getting the ball to him on the edge of the opposition penalty-area where Eric was one of the most dangerous players in the country. He always caused defenders problems and could either lay the ball off or twist and turn and create an opening for a shot. He scored some great goals and set up others where the keeper couldn't hold his shot. Worried defenders would bring him down and we would win penalties and free-kicks right on the edge of penalty-area where Arnold's left foot was deadly.

Defences found the system hard to combat. Either they had to pull a man out of the back four to mark Eric man-to-man which disrupted their system or they had to gamble and leave him free in the hope that he wouldn't get much of the ball. If they pulled a full-back inside they would leave one flank exposed and with runners of Alan Brazil and Paul Mariner's quality we were able to exploit that space. Once opponents were worrying about how we played they had to change their style of play and it was a good psychological blow for us.

The system was unique. No other team in England was using it. We had developed it and we had the players to make it work. Without orthodox wingers, we had players like Arnold and Frans who would push wide and two of the best attacking full-backs in the country in Mick Mills and George Burley who could both hit excellent crosses.

Invariably they would find John Wark. We always tried to get quality balls into the penalty-area, but with the two strikers heavily marked the space was always behind them rather than in front. We were told to pull the crosses back into this space and Warky would time his run perfectly to get on the end of them. He scored most of his goals from this area and this 'late run' has been emulated by other players including Bryan Robson who has developed it to perfection. John is a marvellous lad and a great player. Whenever he got in the box with a half chance he would score. He was very good in the air, had a great eye for an opening and would time his runs immaculately. From 1979 he scored ninety-seven goals for Ipswich in four seasons, which was some measure of his talent and importance to the team.

Initially our results were patchy and it took us time to adapt to this new style of play. Bobby Robson would tell us to be patient. 'Believe in yourselves, keep playing football and the results will come,' he said. But by the end of October during the 1979–80 season we were bottom of the First Division and we were still in the bottom three just before Christmas. Then we beat Manchester City 4–0 at Portman Road and that started us off on a run of twenty-three league games without defeat. Eric Gates scored a hat-trick that day and we could sense that our tactics were going to pay off. We had some marvellous results and won 4–0 at Everton and beat Manchester United 6–0 at Portman Road. They were second in the table when they came to us, but we played them off the park. Gary Bailey saved three penalties that game to save them from further humiliation. Jimmy Nicholl, who's now at Rangers, was in the United team that day and remembers it well.

That evening Russell and I had to join the England Under-21 squad at Heathrow. The man in charge was Dave Sexton, who had just seen us whallop his Manchester United team 6–0 a few hours earlier. Not surprisingly, he was not his normally chirpy self and when Russell and I walked in he said: 'Not you two again: You have caused me enough misery for one day.'

It was quite a season for penalty saves at Portman Road. Paul Cooper saved five that year, including two in one game against Derby County.

I had my most important match of the season in January when I married Rita. We had gone to the same primary school in Lowestoft, and I remember her as one of those children you did not associate with. She was a bit of a rebel and used to hang out with some loud and lively friends. I do not think she was impressed by me either as she says I was a 'tall, skinny boy who ignored girls and was only interested in football.' Luckily we got on better when we met again several years later.

The wedding was on the Sunday after a trip to Bristol

City, where we won my last game as a bachelor 3–0. Russell organized several gallons of scrumpy for the coach ride home. It's a long way to Ipswich from the West Country and we arrived back in fine spirits. Nearly all my team-mates came up to Lowestoft for the reception and I put on a coach to make sure they got home safely. One or two came by car and were stopped by a policeman at Saxmundham on their way back to Ipswich. He immediately smelt their breath and asked where they had been.

'A wedding reception.'

'Oh yes! Who got married?' said the policeman reaching for his notebook and breathalyser.

'Terry Butcher, the Ipswich footballer.'

'Oh, Terry. Well that's all right. I used to go to school with him. On you go sir and drive carefully.'

Rita and I moved to a part of Ipswich which was densely populated with footballers. Within five hundred yards of our house you could find Eric Gates, Kevin O'Callaghan, Steve McCall and John Wark, and Alan Brazil and Russell lived next door to each other just up the road from us. While Rita was working I would spend my spare time gallivanting around with the lads.

After a two-day honeymoon I was back in training and the following Saturday playing football against Bristol City once again, this time in the FA Cup. Goals from John Wark and Paul Mariner gave us a 2–1 victory and in the next round we were at home to Chester City. There was some talk about the young Chester centre-forward who people said was quite useful. His name was Ian Rush and he caused us a few problems then with his pace, but in the end we went through with another 2–1 victory. In those days Ian Rush was skinny and introverted and none of us thought he would go on to cause us so many problems in years to come.

We went to Everton in the sixth round and, having won there 4–0 in the League, we fancied our chances. On the day it wasn't to be. We played badly and lost 2–1. We had already gone out of the League Cup and the UEFA Cup early on and were obviously disappointed to be knocked out of the FA Cup, especially as our League form had been so good at the time. But we had climbed to third place in the table and qualified for Europe again.

I missed the last few games of the season with a broken leg, although I hadn't realized it was broken at the time and played another two games in absolute agony.

I remember picking up a knock in a home game against Coventry. I had scored our first goal in a 3–0 win and was enjoying the game. Shortly after my goal the ball ran loose in front of Paul Dyson. He's a big lad, about six feet tall and thirteen stone, and as we both launched ourselves into the tackle he crashed into my shin. I was in a lot of pain, but I didn't want to show that I was hurt so I hobbled away. That night I went to a dinner and dance with Paul and Ali Mariner, John and Toula Wark and a few of the lads, but the leg was so painful I couldn't stand yet alone dance with Rita. I thought I had damaged my calf muscle and, after receiving treatment all week, played the following Saturday at Southampton where we won 1–0. The leg was still sore and I should have pulled out of the England Under-21 squad, which was leaving to play in East Germany the next week. But it was an important game for me so I kept quiet and prayed that the leg would heal.

I received more treatment in Germany, told Dave Sexton, who was in charge of the team, that I felt fine and played. By half-time we were 1–0 down and I couldn't even walk. I was in so much pain that I was of no use to the team and reluctantly came off. The following day the pain was worse and when I arrived back at Portman Road Bobby Robson exploded. 'Why did you go if you weren't fit?' he said. 'You could have done all kinds of damage.'

They decided to give me an X-ray and found that the calf injury was in fact a clean break of the fibula, the thin bone that runs from the knee to the ankle. That was the end of my season, although the boss still took me away for our end of season to Israel, promoting me to entertainments officer.

I was fit in time for the start of the next season – 1980–1 – and there was a feeling throughout the club that this was to be our year. Our results in the second half of the previous season would make us championship contenders if we could repeat them for forty-two games.

5

The Best Team in Europe

Ipswich's first game in the 1980–1 season was away to Leicester, never normally a good hunting ground for us. It was one of the hottest days of the summer and they had just been promoted so we expected a tough match. We won 1–0 with John Wark scoring ten minutes before the end. An away win early on in the season gives a team a good lift and, although we knew we had nothing to get carried away about yet, that result reinforced the belief that we were on the verge of success.

We won seven of our first eight games. The only point we dropped was at Stoke where two mistakes had let them in for a 2–2 draw when the game had been ours for the taking. Bobby Robson was furious, not only at the way we had played, but because he'd had a bet with a few mates that we would win and two mistakes had cost him his winnings.

Our unbeaten run continued into November ending with an away defeat at Brighton. I missed that game through suspension after being sent-off at Southampton the previous Saturday.

It's always a ding-dong at the Dell and this game was no exception. Soon after setting up a goal for Paul Mariner to give us a 3–2 lead I mistimed a tackle on Steve Williams, the Southampton midfield player. It wasn't a bad tackle but he made a meal out of it and started writhing about in melodramatic style. I knew he was nowhere near as injured as he made out, but what really made me angry was the reaction of the Southampton players.

They surrounded the referee and were shouting at him to send me off. I couldn't believe that fellow professionals would do that but I could hear it for myself. Eventually the referee emerged from the mêlée and pointed to the dressing rooms. For the first time in my career I had been sent off.

People ask me what goes through a player's mind on such an occasion. In my case it was anger, absolute anger. I came into the changing room and kicked a hole in the door, threw my boots across the room and if there had been anything else that was breakable I would have smashed that. I was so wild that even our 6′ 2″ kitman, Trevor Kirton was too scared to console me. I was furious that the referee seemed to be swayed by people on the pitch who wanted me off. I went over the incident time after time in my mind to examine whether I had deserved to go and was convinced I should still be on the pitch, not sitting alone in the changing room.

My mood didn't improve when I heard an almighty roar from the crowd which signalled that Southampton had equalized. I couldn't escape from the game if I had wanted to as they had the radio commentary on in the changing room and there was no way of turning it off. So for the rest of the game I had to listen to the commentators go on and on about my dismissal.

Bobby Ferguson had told me: 'You won't have made it as a centre-half until you are sent-off. It's your job to go after the ball – to try and be a winner.' It was no consolation and I kept thinking about the people I had let down – my team-mates, the supporters and my family, especially my father with his belief in fair play and sporting tradition.

After dropping those three points at Southampton and Brighton we slipped to third place in the League. But wins over Norwich, Forest and Birmingham as we went into the New Year had put us back on top.

Our only disappointment so far that season had been the League Cup. In the first round we were given a shock by Middlesbrough who beat us 3–1 in the first leg. As we left the pitch we could see that their players thought they were already through. But we turned it on at Portman Road and won the second leg 3–0. Russell scored one, Paul Mariner two, and the Middlesbrough players couldn't believe it. Nor could their fans who had made the long journey to Ipswich. They gave their side some stick for throwing away a 3–1 lead. Tony McAndrew wouldn't put up with this and, as we left the pitch, he started a good old argument with some of the more vociferous critics in the stand and had to be guided away by his team-mates.

We beat our East Anglian rivals, Norwich, in the next round after a replay when we went to Carrow Road and won 3–1. Victory over Norwich has always been sweet for me. As a local lad I know how important the result is to the fans. They made it clear they could forgive us for losing to anybody else, but the one team we had to beat was Norwich. The rivalry soon rubbed off on to players who moved into the area, and lads like George Burley and Mick Mills were as keyed up for the 'derby' games as I was. The only player who had any problem was Clive Woods who played nearly three hundred games for us but was born in Norwich, supported Norwich and went on to play for Norwich.

Just as we looked set for a good League Cup run we lost at Birmingham in the fourth round. It was a disappointing result for us as we beat them twice in the League that season. I think every player likes to be involved in a good cup run regardless of whether their team is top or bottom of the League. But we still had the FA Cup to look forward to and in the third round we were drawn at home to Aston Villa. We won another tough game thanks to a marvellous goal from Paul Mariner after a move involving Thijssen, Muhren, Wark and Brazil. We were arguably the two best teams in the country and after the game Bobby Robson said that Villa would be the team to push us for the title.

The newspaper headlines after that game were all about an incident involving Peter Withe, me and a ripped shirt. I had stooped to head a ball that had been played in about waist height. Withey, who was centre-forward for Villa, came in to play it with his feet and I ended up with my shirt ripped and stud marks down my back. There was a lot of fuss Jimmy Hill wanted me to appear on Match of the Day and others were pressing me to say that Withey should have been sent off. It may have looked bad, but as far as I was concerned it was an accident. Withey thanked me later for not kicking up a stink and we ended up as room-mates in the World Cup in Spain and firm friends ever since.

I prefer marking a player like Peter Withe. If they throw their weight around it keeps you on your toes. Peter is a hard man and a fierce competitor. He's all elbows and awkward to play against, but for a big man he has a good touch. We came out even over our tussles and Peter can take stick as well as dish it out. Critics often overlook his skill and he also has a sharp brain and takes up some excellent positions. I'm sure he was responsible for much of Villa's success around that time.

Not many First Division sides fancy a trip to a small, lower division club and Shrewsbury was to prove a hazardous ground for us over the next few years. We met them in the fourth round that season and they packed 18,000 fans into Gay Meadow squashing them right up against the pitch. It created a frenetic atmosphere which was reflected in the football with neither side able to put together more than three passes before giving the ball away. We were lucky to get a 0–0 draw and had another blow when George Burley injured his knee ligaments. It put him out of football for the next ten months and we lost the services of the best right-back in the League.

We won the replay 3–0 and, after beating Charlton 2–0 in the fifth round, were one game away from the semi-finals. People were already starting to talk about Wembley and our form was so good that we were being tipped for the treble of League, FA Cup and UEFA Cup.

Confidence was sky high as we ran out for our sixth round game against Nottingham Forest at the City Ground. We went 2–0 up before Forest staged a remarkable recovery to level the scores and then go into the lead after the referee, Clive Thomas, awarded a controversial penalty – most things Clive did were controversial! This time he said John Wark deliberately handled a cross from John Robertson even though Warky was less than five or six feet from Robertson when he crossed and had no chance to get out of the way.

With time running out we equalized with one of the luckiest goals I have ever seen. Frans Thijssen hit a shot from the edge of the area which Peter Shilton in the Forest goal had covered until a wicked deflection carried it into the other corner. It's the kind of luck you get when you are on a good run and it was enough to save a game that we had looked like throwing away. After the match some of the Ipswich officials went to say goodbye to Brian Clough and found him stunned, sitting in his office with Peter Taylor and Kenny Burns in complete darkness.

In the replay Forest were superb for the first twenty minutes but couldn't find the net. We came back and Arnold Muhren scored the only goal – a rare right-foot volley – which was enough to put us through to the semi-finals. It was a marvellous feeling. Every year I had watched the FA Cup Final on TV and thought about how much I would like to be there. Now we were just one game away.

The FA Cup is the competition that captures everyone's imagination. The supporters start singing about Wembley from the third round and thousands more come to away games if they are in the Cup. It's important for Ipswich because of the success in 1978. The fans remember the great times of that season and can't wait for them to happen again.

The talk about the treble continued. When it is in the papers nearly every day it's impossible for the players to ignore it and although some people thought it affected us I don't think it put us under any greater pressure. I know it's a cliché, but we really did take each game as it came.

Our League form had slipped slightly with away defeats at Manchester United, Leeds and West Brom. Manchester City, our semi-final opponents, were in mid-table, and only had the Cup to play for so we knew it would be tough.

The game was at Villa Park and we stayed at a hotel just outside Birmingham. Before a big game players like to have a good night's sleep. We had struck it unlucky that night. First we were awoken by a fire alarm just after midnight then we were kept awake by ducks quacking outside the bedroom window.

At the pre-match meal Bobby Robson said Kevin Beattie would be playing and I would be left-back. I had a week's growth in the hope a beard may have made me look fearsome, but if the City players knew what I was feeling inside they would have found that I was more nervous than before any other game in my career.

It suddenly hit me how much this game meant, not only to the team, but to the thousands of supporters who had either travelled to Birmingham or were following the game on the radio at home.

The game whizzed by. We had the chances but couldn't score and in the eighty-sixth minute we lost Kevin Beattie with a broken arm. It was still 0–0 but losing Beattie was a severe blow as he had looked our most dangerous player. I moved to centre-half and in extra-time I had a free-kick given against me for a foul on Dave Bennett. I thought it was a fair challenge, but from the free-kick Paul Power bent a shot past Paul Cooper for the only goal of the game.

As the ball went in a terrible chill came over us. There was a sudden hush from the supporters in the Ipswich end which was even more noticeable than the noise being made by the celebrating City fans. For the first time the thought flashed through my mind that we could lose.

When a team scores their hopes are lifted, their players seem fresh and they start to buzz. If you concede a goal your spirits drop, your legs feel heavy, you find it hard to move, passes go astray and things start to go wrong. We couldn't get going again. Our attacks had little idea behind them and we started pumping long balls forward in hope rather than with any purpose. So much depended on whether we won or lost that desperation took over.

They say that losing a semi-final is harder than losing a final. I can believe that as I have never been so dejected as I was after that game. We hadn't played well, but still should have won. I was so disappointed that I couldn't bring myself to watch the Final between Manchester City and Spurs. Instead, Rita and I decorated a bedroom at our new house. We had beaten Tottenham at Portman Road that season and I felt sure we would have beaten them again at Wembley. In the end Ricky Villa scored that marvellous goal in the replay to maintain Tottenham's record of never having lost an FA Cup Final.

Three days after the semi-final we returned to Villa Park, this time to play Villa in a vital League match. We needed to win to keep our title hopes alive. Villa, our main rivals for the championship, were obviously hoping to catch us with a hangover from the semi-final. Strangely enough that defeat had given us a new determination and we played some great football and won 2–1. You could see that the Villa players thought they had lost the championship there and then. Tony

Morley, their winger, said to me after the game: 'That's it, we've blown it now.'

It was the tonic we needed. We still had the chance of a League and European double, with the second leg of our UEFA Cup semi-final just seven days away. Our European run had been full of incident. In the first round the Greek side Aris Salonika had three booked and one sent off as we won the first leg 5–1. John Wark scored four, including three penalties. Some of their challenges were a little over enthusiastic and Eric Gates in particular finished the game with his legs covered in bruises.

The Greek press is supposed to have given the impression that Salonika were cheated out of the game in England. When we went there about 3,000 hostile Salonika fans turned out to spit, jeer and hurl stones at us while we trained.

The hospitality didn't improve much for the game. We kicked off at two o'clock in the afternoon which was the hottest part of the day, and it was obvious they were doing everything they could to give themselves as big an advantage as possible. The pitch was hard and bumpy and the touch-lines seemed to be about a foot thick. It was apparent things were going to be difficult when Mick Mills twice cleared the ball before it crossed the line and the referee signalled a goal both times. The officials seemed to be turning a blind eye to some of the Greek challenges and we were continuously kicked, punched and elbowed.

Twenty minutes into the second-half they scored a third which we felt should have been disallowed for a foul on Paul Cooper. Suddenly our 5–1 lead from the first leg looked vulnerable. They needed one more to level the aggregate and they would be ahead on away goals. But eight minutes later Eric Gates popped up with a left foot shot that crept in the corner to make the tie safe. Once again he'd taken the brunt of the Greek violence. Eric never wore shinguards and in the treatment room his legs looked like a woodcutters block.

After the game our coach was bombarded with stones and one rock crashed through the window narrowly missing George Burley. However, we saw a nicer side of the country that evening. John Wark's wife had relatives in Greece and they took us for a splendid traditional Greek meal which left a much better taste in the mouth than had the game against Salonika.

Our next opponents were Bohemians Prague and once again we were at home in the first leg. We were 2–0 up with five minutes to go when Kevin Beattie came on as substitute and scored with his first touch – a spectacular shot from a free-kick. It was to prove a vital goal.

Kevin was dominant in the second leg in Prague which was played in sub zero temperatures. Bohemians scored once in each half but our three goal lead was too much for them to overcome. Crowds in Communist countries in eastern Europe are normally quiet, but in Prague they were quite animated and gave the game a bit of atmosphere. The city though was like a ghost town when we drove through it in the evening with dark, empty streets and no sign of night life.

We faced another east European team in the third round. Widzew Lodz of Poland had already put out Juventus and Manchester United, were top of the Polish League and had some world class players like Boniek and Zmuda. Again the first leg was at Portman Road and we played superbly winning 5–0 with another hat-trick for John Wark and Paul Mariner and Alan Brazil scoring the others.

I don't think I have ever been so cold as I was during the return trip to Poland. We flew to Warsaw and had to travel to Lodz by road. It was December, temperatures were between minus 15° and minus 20° centigrade and there was no heating on the coach. The players were huddled together in winter coats, hats, scarves and anything else that would keep us warm.

We trained on the Lodz pitch on the night before the game. There was a thin layer of snow on top which was enough to take a stud, but underneath it was hard packed ice. The next day it snowed and the temperature plummeted even further. The Lodz groundstaff tried to clear the pitch by driving a tractor across it pulling a chain to move the snow. It was hopeless. The pitch was even worse with icy ruts carved out by the tractor's wheels. If it was a League game in Britain it would never have gone ahead.

Some of the players wore track suit bottoms, others wore tights, padding and two or three shirts and most had mittens. I didn't feel comfortable with more than one shirt on so I wore a long sleeved top. Kevin Beattie reckoned we were all soft and came on as substitute wearing a short-sleeved shirt. Once again he was magnificent and played his heart out as though he was quite used to the conditions.

We lost 1–0 but were never in danger of losing the tie. We were due to fly home that evening and faced a three-hour drive back to Warsaw airport. The roads were treacherous so our kit man, Trevor Kirton, set off immediately after the game to make sure the baggage was checked through customs to avoid any delay when we arrived at the airport.

Once again our coach had no heating and it was so cold ice had formed on the inside of the windows. Most of the lads had bought duty free sherry, port and brandy on the way out to stock up for Christmas, but we were so cold we drank the lot there and then.

Before long we were warmed up and singing Christmas carols. Alan Brazil had a great voice and led us through a selection of Beatles hits and Rolling Stones songs and we had a good old knees up. Our Polish interpreter couldn't make us out at all.

On the road we passed a truck which had skidded into a ditch. There were a few people scurrying around trying to push it back on the road and we gave them a cheer as we passed. An hour later we saw a truck in a ditch on the other side of the road.

At the airport we saw Trevor Kirton who looked frozen. 'Are we glad to be here in one piece,' we said. 'The roads are terrible, we saw two trucks that had skidded off.'

'I know,' said Trevor. 'I was in them. I saw you drive past both times without picking me up.' He said he had dislocated his shoulder in the first accident and was still in pain when they pushed the truck back on the road and continued their journey. When it went into the ditch the second time, the heavy landing jolted the shoulder back into place!

It was during that trip to Poland that we heard that John Lennon had been killed. I was shocked by the news. He had been a great hero, not only to me but to millions of people around my age and his death, like that of Elvis Presley, stunned music lovers everywhere.

When the European competitions resumed in March we were paired with St Etienne, one of the best teams in France with players like Platini, Larios and Johnny Rep. They had already beaten St Mirren and had trounced Hamburg 6–0 on aggregate, winning 5–0 in Germany. We knew it would be tough, especially playing the first leg of the quarter-final in France.

We had beaten Coventry 4–0 at Highfield Road on the Saturday before so we flew out full of confidence. Russell and I went off to explore the town and found a small bar where we settled down for a few glasses of the local brew. We arrived back at the hotel in time for the meal and noticed that we weren't the only players to find comfort in a local hostelry. No one had gone mad, but several of the other lads had a slight slur to their voices. It was ideal preparation as there is nothing worse than feeling as though you are a prisoner in a hotel and unable to leave the grounds.

The Geoffroy-Guichard stadium in St Etienne was packed about an hour and a half before kick-off with thousands more locked out. When we went on to the pitch there were 42,000 Frenchmen singing and chanting and making a tremendous noise. When they saw us they started throwing anything they could lay their hands on and apples, oranges and cans came raining down. Ever the joker, Russell picked up an orange and started bowling it back into the crowd which incensed them even more.

I could sense before the game that our attitude was right and that we were going to do well. Even after St Etienne went ahead I knew it was going to be our night. The St Etienne players had been jubilant after that early goal from Johnny Rep and you could see they were thinking that they would notch up another couple before half-time. But we came back and played some great football. We went close several times before Paul Mariner scored to make it 1–1 at half-time. It was the first goal they had conceded in Europe that season and with an away goal being so important we went in for the break sky high while we could see they were devastated.

I was left-back again and marking a nippy winger. He sped past me early on and I thought: 'Oh no, I've got my hands full here.' But a couple of firm tackles, using all fourteen stone and he never came near me again. I spent more of the game attacking him than he did attacking me.

The Ipswich fans in the crowd were making themselves heard in the second half and we played some inspired football. Our second goal was brilliant, an Arnold Muhren shot from twenty-five yards which swerved and went in off the post. I had a hand in the third, almost scoring from an Alan Brazil cross, the ball coming back off the keeper for Paul Mariner to knock home. We were cock-a-hoop and when John Wark scored a fourth with a powerful header from the edge of the area it put the seal on a magnificent team performance.

In thirty European ties, St Etienne had lost only twice at home. Their fans, who had jeered us early on, applauded us off the pitch. At last we had shown everyone what we could do.

In Europe we played basically the same system that we had developed at home, with Eric Gates in the hole behind the strikers. If need be he would come back into more of a midfield role which would give us an orthodox 4–4–2 system and was useful if we were under pressure. But when we broke Eric would be the first to be released and help the forwards.

The system may be out of date now, but it worked a treat for that side. As a centre-half I know how difficult it was to play against because you are always worried about what was going on in front of you and who was going to pick up the man in Eric's position.

The flight home from St Etienne that evening was one long party and the celebrations continued through the night. Russell's father, Rex, ran the Centre Spot restaurant at the Ipswich ground and he put on a special meal for a few of the lads at Russell's house. Much to Rita's annoyance I rolled home in the early hours of the morning blind drunk.

The festivities continued the next day with a lunch at the Belstead Brook Hotel. Since 1978 it had been a tradition at Ipswich to have a players' lunch on the Thursday before an FA Cup tie and we were playing Forest in the sixth round two days later. Most of the lads were drinking orange juice, but Russell and I were friendly with the manager, Ian Hatfield, who kept slipping vodkas in ours to help us savour that victory a little longer.

St Etienne knew the second leg was a formality. We were determined not to waste the good work we had done and I scored the first goal in a 3–1 win. We had beaten some of the best teams in Europe and now faced the crack German side Cologne in the semi-finals.

Cologne had a good team which included Tony Woodcock, who had joined them from Nottingham Forest, Rene Betteron, the Swiss international and an array of German internationals including Toni Schumacher, Rainer Bonhof, Pierre Littbarski and Dieter Muller. They were a typical, well-disciplined German team who were fit and could knock the ball around well but they didn't seem too adventurous.

We won the difficult first leg at Ipswich by the only goal, a John Wark header. The papers were saying it wouldn't be enough in Germany and that we were as good as out. The lads weren't nearly as despondent. We had won and, just as importantly, we hadn't conceded a goal.

Over the next ten days our world started to fall apart. We lost that FA Cup semi-final against Manchester City and, although we had beaten Villa to put ourselves back in with a good chance in the League, we had thrown away any advantage of losing at home to Arsenal. Two days later we lost at Norwich. That was a disaster. Bobby Robson told us after that game that we had blown the championship. Norwich went down that season and the game had been there for us to win.

We flew to Germany from Norwich airport straight after the game. People were so low that hardly anyone said anything and most of the lads went to bed without a beer. Our only chance of a trophy now was the UEFA Cup and we had two days to lift ourselves before the second leg of the semi-final.

To help us relax we went to a theme park which gave us a day away from football and was the perfect break. Most of us went on the roller-coaster and I couldn't help thinking how symbolic it was of our season. As soon as we reached the top we came hurtling down again and when we reached the bottom we started to climb once more. I prayed we would rise again against Cologne.

There was a big crowd, almost 55,000, with a sizeable Ipswich contingent which was swollen by some British soldiers based in Germany. They gave us a terrific reception. Paul Cooper and Russell Osman were outstanding in the first half as Cologne put us under pressure, and the game was finely balanced at o–o when twenty minutes after half-time we won a free-kick midway into the Cologne half. I had pushed up into their penalty-area and when Mick Mills slightly under-hit it I had to stoop to get a touch. My glance had sent the ball goalwards but it seemed to be heading for the post until it bounced and span in. Schumacher never moved. I couldn't believe it.

I was thinking: 'I've scored! What's going on?' Then it hit me and I was off. I thought 'I'll have a run like all the others do when they score', and I was away. No one could catch me.

That goal settled it and we flew home to another celebration with Russell's dad. No matter what level of football you play it's always a thrill to be through to a final, especially for us after being so low two days earlier at Norwich.

The party lasted through the night and at six o'clock there was only Russell, me and a crate of lager left. Russell said: 'Come on, let's go and sit outside.'

It was a lovely morning, with a crisp frost, the air was clear and the sun was slowly rising, so we took the crate and two dining-room chairs and sat on the lawn. Russell woke his neighbour, Roger, who initially thought he had burglars, but after a bit of persuasion he came down and joined us.

It wasn't long before people started getting up and going to work. One of my neighbours walked past just before seven o'clock in his overalls and carrying a Thermos flask.

'Morning Terry,' he said.

'Morning.'

'Good win last night lads,' and he continued on his way to work as though it was normal for him to pass two men in overcoats and gloves and a third in his dressing gown and slippers, sitting on the lawn surrounded by empty lager bottles at that time of day.

It was typical of Russell who is always game for a laugh. We had developed a great partnership at the heart of the Ipswich defence and had been good mates since the youth team. Bobby Robson said we went together like bacon and eggs and another footballing gourmet said we were as compatible as oysters and champagne.

On the pitch Russell is an extremely hard and aggressive competitor and most of the time all I had to do was pick up the loose balls behind him. Being great friends helped our understanding. Off the pitch we were inseparable, spending hours playing golf, squash and snooker together. Rita wasn't too keen on him when I eventually came home after the Cologne game, she wasn't too keen on me either at the time, but we were delighted when he was godfather of our eldest son Christopher.

Despite losing to Arsenal and Norwich we still had a chance in the League and I scored my second goal in a week to give us a 1–0 win over Manchester City and set up a grandstand finish for the championship. Our last two games were away to Middlesbrough and at home to Southampton. If Villa slipped and we took maximum points the title could still be ours. But the dream faded at Ayresome Park. Despite Paul Mariner giving us a half-time lead Middlesbrough came back, inspired by Bosko Jankovic who scored twice to give them the points. The lads were devastated. Arsenal had beaten Villa but we had failed with a poor second-half performance. I'll always remember that long drive home down the A1. The players were so miserable but the boss and Fergie were doing their best to lift our spirits for the UEFA Cup Final.

After all the talk about the treble, the UEFA Cup was the only trophy left for us that season and following the disappointments in the League and FA Cup we were determined not to let this one slip. In the final we met AZ Alkmaar, who were the Dutch champions that season.

More than 27,000 fans turned up at Portman Road for the first leg and saw us score three marvellous goals. AZ never got going.

Some pundits were saying that a three-goal lead was easily enough and the cup was as good as ours. Bobby Robson, though, made sure nobody became over confident for the second leg, especially when we let Southampton score three goals in forty-five minutes, days before we were due to fly to Holland. He was livid. 'If Southampton can score three against you so can AZ and the tie will be back in the melting pot,' he said.

There were plenty of people at the club who remembered earlier European ties where Ipswich lost a three goal lead to Barcelona going out on penalties, and against Bruges who beat us 4–0 in the second leg.

The game was played on a hot, sticky May evening at the impressive Olympic stadium in Amsterdam. As we left our hotel for the ground, Mick Mills, Paul Cooper, Eric Gates and Alan Brazil became stuck in a lift for twenty minutes. They were squashed together and nearly roasted before they were freed. The delay put the rest of us on edge and must have been frightening for them.

The Ipswich fans had been marvellous all season and more than 6,000 travelled to Holland including my mother and father and Rita. When we walked on to the pitch there was a huge bank of blue and white. Some people had spent a fortune following us that season and we were determined not to let them down this time.

We had a great start when Frans Thijssen scored after four minutes. It meant AZ had to score at least five to beat us. Russell looked at me and said: 'It's got to be all over now.'

However, AZ came back at us grabbing an equalizer three minutes later and then taking the lead through Johnny Metgod. John Wark levelled the score on the night, which meant AZ now needed to score six but they showed no sign of throwing in the towel and scored a third before half-time.

The manager and Bobby Ferguson were going mad trying to re-organize us and calm us down. AZ Alkmaar had thrown caution to the wind and were pushing everyone into attack. We pulled as many back as we could leaving only Alan Brazil and Paul Mariner on the half-way line. 'Don't do anything stupid,' said the boss. 'There's only forty-five minutes to go.'

AZ kept attacking and scored a fourth twenty minutes from time. We had a few scares but survived to become the first British side to win the UEFA Cup since Liverpool in 1976.

When the whistle went there was pandemonium as thousands of fans poured on to the pitch to join in the celebrations. I made straight for Johnny Metgod who had impressed me enormously. He is still a world class player with Nottingham Forest. I thought it would be a coup to swap my shirt with him when a Dutch fan whipped it off me and ran away. The shirt meant as much to me as a medal so, oblivious to the hugging and congratulations going on around me, I raced through the crowd and caught the thief. I did not speak Dutch so I just growled: 'You give that shirt here, pal.' I must have looked as though I meant business because he handed it back immediately.

We had wanted to do a lap of honour but there were so many fans on the pitch it was impossible. Mick Mills and Eric Gates, the two smallest men in our team had the huge cup in the middle of the pitch and were in danger of being swamped. I thought 'Blow this', so I snatched the cup and battled my way through the mob to the safety of the dressing room. The champagne was flowing and at last I had my hands on a winner's medal.

6

How I Nearly Died

There aren't many things a footballer fears more than picking up a serious injury. I've had my share including two broken cheekbones and a series of knee injuries, but my darkest moment came on a blustery, overcast afternoon at Luton on 23 January 1982. It seemed harmless at the time; a boot in the face which is the kind of knock you have to live with as a centre-half. But two days later I was rushed to hospital and was kept in for five weeks. The doctors told me later that they thought I was going to die.

It was the fourth round of the FA Cup and I was marking Brian Stein, the Luton forward. A ball was played into him which he didn't control, and as it popped up off his thigh I could see John Wark in space and bent forward to head the ball towards him. At the same time Stein tried an overhead kick and I felt a tremendous crack on the side of my face as he caught me with his boot.

There was blood everywhere and a huge lump came up on the side of my nose. It was obviously broken but I carried on with a sponge to try and stop the bleeding. At half-time, the Ipswich physio, Tommy Eggleston, packed my nose with cotton wool. The bleeding stopped and with the game still wide open I went out for the second half.

We went two up, but the game was still in the balance when the plugs burst and blood poured out. Clive Thomas was the referee and asked if I wanted to go off. I said I was fine and Tommy gave me some more cotton wool to try and block it.

Nosebleeds normally stop after a few minutes but this was getting worse and I was swallowing blood with every breath.

Every time I headed the ball I was losing more blood and I was starting to struggle. With about fifteen minutes to go we scored a third to make the game safe and Bobby Robson signalled for me to come off. I went straight to the Luton physio room where they tried every trick in the First Aid book to stop the bleeding. I had ice on my nose, I held my breath and I sat, stood and knelt with my head in a variety of positions before the bleeding stopped more than two hours later.

The rest of the lads had gone back to Ipswich, but my father had been at the game with some friends so he drove Tommy and me to the local hospital. An X-ray confirmed the break and the doctors gave me some padding and bandages in case the bleeding started again.

On the way home we stopped for a McDonalds. I was still wearing my Ipswich kit and sat in the corner in a blood-stained shirt looking a terrible state. The other customers gave us some odd glances and, as if that wasn't embarrassing enough, my father kicked up a fuss because he couldn't find the knives and forks! He'd never been in a McDonalds before and didn't realize you eat without them.

The next day I thought the worst was over. I went out for lunch with Rita and Russell, enjoyed an abundance of red wine and in the afternoon everyone came round to our house. It was a lovely relaxing Sunday. But that night the horror story began. I woke up and could feel the pressure mounting behind my nose. I just made it to the bathroom before the plugs burst and blood streamed out rather like a dam bursting.

It didn't stop. Rita phoned for a taxi and insisted that I go to hospital. I sat in the back with a plastic washing up bowl in my lap to collect the blood. It's not a long journey, but the bowl was nearly full by the time we arrived at casualty. I was kept in overnight.

The doctors said I had damaged an artery and kept me in for a few days before they decided to operate. It checked the bleeding for a while, but suddenly and violently it started again. Over the next eight days I lost roughly nine pints of blood so they decided to transfer me to the London hospital in Whitechapel for further X-rays and intensified treatment.

I was beginning to worry. My nose was bleeding heavily for two or three hours at a time. Whenever it stopped I would lie back with such relief then, all of a sudden, it would come back with the horrible sensation of blood trickling down my throat. Once again I would have to sit up for another long session with my head over a kidney bowl to catch the deluge.

It contined like this day after day. I lost almost sixteen pints of blood and two stone in weight. My fingers were so thin that my wedding ring kept falling off. I hadn't shaved and when my dad came to see me he said I looked like an old man. I felt I was withering away.

The doctors continued their tests, but I seemed to be getting worse instead of better. They said they would like to put some dye in my veins and take some X-rays. The dye would have to be injected into my neck and groin.

On the morning of the injections a man in a white coat came along and said he had to shave me. I thought he meant my face and said fine.

'Right,' he said, 'lift up the bedclothes.'

'I beg your pardon!'

'I've got to shave you, take your night-shirt off please.'

It slowly dawned on me what he meant. 'You're joking,' I said, 'You don't mean down there?'

'Yes, down there,' he said and pulled out a cut throat razor which he started sharpening on a leather strap. I lay back and prayed that he had a steady hand. It's a terrible experience for a man, especially when he's only in hospital for treatment to his nose.

I showed Rita his handiwork and all she could do was laugh. I didn't find it funny at the time. I didn't mind what else they did, but to shave me around there was a loss of male dignity.

I had the X-ray and more tests and they explained that a piece of bone had severed an artery and, as my arteries were unusually large, it was difficult to patch up.

There were times when I thought it would never end. They tried injecting a clotting agent into my veins but the bleeding continued. The surgeons told my parents that they were worried. Unless the bleeding stopped soon there was a danger that I could die. The only hope was an operation to tie off the artery but it was extremely risky. And I had been given so many transfusions that they thought my body might reject any more.

One night things were so bad that I pleaded and begged with the doctors until eventually they agreed to operate. Afterwards the specialist said the bleeding would continue for a while but they hoped it would stop eventually. I was feeling so low. The operation improved things but I still had nose bleeds every four or five hours.

The Ipswich fans had been marvellous and sent me hundreds of get well cards, which I have kept in an album to this day. They cheered me up no end but one day a letter arrived which really caught my eye.

It was from a faith healer who had read about my plight and he and his friends had sent me a blue-and-white handker-chief. The letter said: 'We have prayed for you and blessed this handkerchief. Put it to your nose at eight o'clock in the evening: we will be praying for you at that time and the bleeding will stop. At other times wear the handkerchief in the top pocket of your pyjamas.'

My first reaction was to think it was a load of rubbish, but the bleeding was continuing and I thought it was worth a try. I put the handkerchief in my pocket and at eight o'clock I held it to my nose. Astonishingly from that moment it never bled again.

Although the nose had shown signs that it was healing after the operation, the bleeding had continued sporadically until the message from the faith healers. I had been sceptical before but I will never dismiss them as rubbish again.

I had lost so much strength that I faced a long road to full fitness. I set myself targets which I would try and beat each day. I started with a walk around the ward, which was an achievement at the time, then I would try and walk down the corridor and back. Within a few days I could walk down the stairs and look out of the front door. When I felt the fresh air it was a wonderful moment; I had almost forgotten what it was like after being in hospital for more than five weeks.

I started to regain my appetite. My sister Vanda and her husband Nigel worked in the Samuel Pepys pub which over-looks the River Thames in London and when they came to visit they brought huge crispy French loaves filled with chicken, lettuce and tomato. I would finish my hospital meal and then tuck into these. Rita and my mother had stayed in London and visited me every afternoon. They would smuggle in extra food parcels and I began to put on weight again.

Brian Stein had sent a telegram and phoned regularly to ask how I was progressing, which was nice. The kick had been an accident and there was no way that Brian could be blamed for what happened.

I couldn't wait to get home and back to Portman Road so I could see the lads and be part of the scene again. When you're injured you can often feel as though you are an outsider and I was desperate to start training and become involved once more. To build me up the doctors gave me iron tablets and told me to drink Guinness. I thought this was a great suggestion so I was out every night for a couple of pints and enjoying the taste of beer again after five weeks of hospital tea.

When I went back to the ground I was thin and weak and had trouble jogging once round the practice pitch. Tommy Eggleston took me under his wing and we started with a few general exercises and gradually built it up day by day. It was short and sharp and nothing to tire me. I could feel myself getting stronger by the day and, after my exercises, he would see how far I could run in five minutes. He timed me round the practice pitch and each day I improved. It was hard work but I was determined to do it.

Watching the lads training acted as a great spur. They were still challenging for the title so there was an even greater incentive to get fit and try and regain my place in the team.

I made good progress and four weeks after leaving hospital I began my comeback, coming on as substitute for the reserves against Fulham. I was pushed into midfield to give me a run out for forty-five minutes. I am hopeless in midfield and the game seemed to pass me by, but we scrambled a goal for a 1-0 victory and I was delighted to go home with a £2 win bonus. I felt exhausted but a few days later I played a full game against Crystal Palace reserves and we won 7-0. Paul Mariner was also making his comeback after an Achilles tendon operation and we helped each other through our lonely training session.

I was feeling stronger with each game and played again against Tottenham reserves who had Terry Gibson in their side. He's only five feet five inches tall, nearly a foot shorter than me, but somehow he back-headed me full force on my nose. It started bleeding immediately and I thought: 'Oh, God, no, here we go again.' I had visions of the nightmare starting once more. Straight after the game I rushed to see the specialist who luckily reassured me and told me I had nothing to worry about. The latest bang had stopped bleeding and had nothing to do with the previous injury. And he said that there shouldn't be any more problems because the nose would now be stronger.

Things were looking up. On 7 April 1982 Rita gave birth to Christopher our first son. I was as proud as punch. A week later I was called into the first team for the game against West Ham. It was just over six weeks since I had come out of hospital and Rita thought I was coming back too soon. But I think I surprised a lot of people with the speed of my recovery. I am the sort of person who has to get back and play quickly and, although I was tired after the game, I came through quite well and we won 3–2. It was a tribute to Tommy Eggleston whose patience and guidance had helped me return so soon.

We went on to win seven of our last nine games in a stirring finish to the 1981–82 season, but once again we were pipped for the title, this time by Liverpool. On the last Saturday of the season we lost 3–1 at home to Nottingham Forest. They had Steve Hodge and Peter Davenport up front who murdered us. Liverpool won that day so were League champions whatever our result. It was the second season running we had finished as runners-up. All that hard work, and once again we had nothing to show for it.

As we sat in the changing room I felt empty, and as I looked around I could see that the other lads looked totally drained. We should have been celebrating finishing so high but we had set our sights on the title and anything less was a disappointment.

Bobby Robson tried to lift us. 'Never mind lads,'he said. 'We've had a good season.' He must have felt as low as the rest of us.

Why didn't Ipswich win more? It's hard to put your finger on one reason, but the players must take responsibility. In 1980–81 we were so close to winning the championship, but lost seven of our last ten games. That's not the form that wins trophies. We played sixty-six games that season and towards the end we had a crucial match every three or four days. We seemed to reserve our worst performances for the most vital stage of the season and we never seemed to be firing on all cylinders.

If we had won the FA Cup semi-final against Manchester City I think we would have gone on to win the League. It would have given us a boost at the right time. Key players like George Burley and Kevin Beattie were unavailable through injury towards the end of the season and we obviously missed their experience.

In 1981–82 we were again hit by injuries. George Burley missed the first couple of months with the knee injury he picked up the previous season; I was out for nearly three months; Paul Mariner missed seventeen League games with an Achilles tendon injury; and Frans Thijssen broke his leg against Liverpool and made only twelve League appearances all season.

Bobby Robson and Bobby Ferguson had performed wonders in building a team to challenge for major honours while maintaining a happy, family atmosphere at the club. They worked well together. Fergie was often left in charge of the coaching. He deserves a lot of credit. He is a shrewd tactician who can look at a side and spot faults and weaknesses which we used to exploit.

Bobby Robson commanded enormous respect from the players and we had a lot of faith in him. What he said went, especially when players asked for a pay rise at the end of the season. He used to ask them what they thought they were worth, then laugh at their reply. He would arrange to see you in his office. 'Well, son, what can I do for you?' he would ask. 'I'd like a rise please, boss'

'What, you must be joking', and he would launch into a long speech about the recession, unemployment, falling gates, inflation and the problems of keeping a football club afloat. It was the same speech each year. After this tale of woe you expected a wage cut and when he said the board would offer you an extra £20 a week, you gratefully accepted it before he changed his mind. It was only when you left his office you realized it was far less than you originally asked for.

Robson also loved to join in the five-a-sides, and still does with the England team. It is unlucky for the side that picks him as he is not the most mobile of players, but he is as competitive as any of us and after one tackle Kenny Sansom needed stitches on his shin.

Bobby Robson told me to watch Hunter and Beattie play if I wanted to model myself on good defenders. I learnt a lot, and for a time they were the best in the land.

Big Allan Hunter taught me a great deal about the art of defensive play. He was a fine judge of when to tackle and when to back off and a superb header of the ball. When he had time he would always look to use the ball and build from the back, but he also knew there were times when you had to be satisfied with the big boot into touch. He would play to the crowd and, never content with rolling the ball off for a throw-in, he would try to clear it over the stand. The crowd loved it, and if he succeeded in lofting the ball out of the ground he would get one of the biggest cheers of the afternoon.

Allan may have looked mean and uncompromising on the pitch, but off it he was one of the most gentle and warm-hearted people I have ever met.

In December 1981 Kevin Beattie was forced to retire from the game at the age of twenty-eight. It was a tragedy for him, for the club and for football in general. When people ask me who was my favourite player I always say it was Kevin Beattie.

He was a marvellous player, strong, quick and unbeatable in the air. He scored thirty-two goals for Ipswich in 296 games, which is a good strike rate for a defender. He deserved more than the nine caps he won for England.

Kevin loved his football and there was no greater sight than seeing him jump to meet a cross and power home a header. He could head a ball with as much force as some people could kick it. And he had tremendous spring. We had an exercise at Ipswich where you stand against a wall and mark the highest point you can reach with your arms stretched above your head. Then you jump and see how much higher you can reach from a standing start. Kevin would win easily every time.

Kevin was a lovely character who loved a laugh and a joke and always made younger players feel at ease. Before training he would sneak off for a crafty smoke with Allan Hunter. If there was a team meeting and someone noticed they were missing one of us would have to rush round to the groundsman's hut where they would be stretched out enjoying a couple of cigarettes and a cup of tea.

Kevin Beattie's dad, Tom, was an even greater character. Often we would be in the changing rooms at away games and shortly before kick-off a head would pop round the door and ask: 'Is Kevin Beattie here?'

'Aye, I'm here.'

'Your dad's outside and wants to see you.'

And Kevin would go out and find his dad blind drunk. We'd hunt around and find a complimentary ticket and Kevin would find someone to look after his dad and put him back on a train to Carlisle, where the Beatties lived.

Kevin was such a strong player that he broke two or three players legs purely through the force of his tackle. However, he was never nasty. Kenny Clements of Manchester City was on the receiving end once. The doctors thought he had been hit by a train the break was so bad, but it had just been a typical Beattie block tackle.

It was typical of Kevin to wear a short-sleeved shirt in a game played in a temperature of minus 15°C. He didn't feel pain. For instance, he always wore long studs, even on hard pitches. Everyone else would have moulded boots to avoid blisters, but you could hear him clip-clopping around oblivious to pain and discomfort.

Kevin was such an important part of the team that he often played when he wasn't fully fit. Perhaps he played in too many games like this. Cortisone injections can ease the pain during a game, but can disguise the greater damage that can be caused by playing with an injury. But that was Kevin. He would never complain and was always willing to play his heart out.

I owe both Allan and Kevin a tremendous amount. They were always willing to offer advice to myself and Russell even though we were pushing to keep them out of the first team.

Kevin Beattie should have played for England in the World Cup in Spain in 1982. Instead, after six operations on his knee, he retired six months before the competition started. It's ironic that as his career ended I should be given my chance in the position he should have filled in the England team.

7

England in Spain

I was driving home when the news came on the car radio. The last item caught my attention.

'And finally, the England manager, Ron Greenwood, has announced his squad of twenty-two players for the World Cup Finals in Spain.' The newsreader paused, my heart pounded in a mixture of fear and anticipation. 'It's Anderson, Brooking, Butcher ...'

I could hardly believe it. 'I'm in,' I kept saying to myself. 'I'm in.' Three months earlier my whole career had been in jeopardy. I had lain in my hospital bed after my second blood transfusion and wondered if I would ever play for Ipswich again. Now I was off to Spain and the World Cup Finals, the greatest stage on which any footballer can appear.

My parents were the first to phone and congratulate me. I could sense how proud they felt. My only sadness was that Russell Osman wasn't in the squad. We had come so far together, from the Ipswich youth side to the full England team, and I was very disappointed our partnership couldn't continue in Spain.

My inclusion surprised a lot of people, including myself. I had only returned to the Ipswich first team in the middle of April after missing three months of the season through the injury to my nose. One week later I was named in the England squad for the Home International against Wales. I was flabbergasted. I didn't even know the squad was being named. I had played only two games in three months and was still trying to build up my strength again. But Alvin Martin, the West Ham defender, was injured and I was in the squad.

I had been out of the England team for more than a year after winning just two caps. My first game was against Australia in Sydney in June 1980. We won 2–1 with goals from Paul Mariner and Glenn Hoddle. We were sent as a makeshift side while the full England squad prepared for the European championships, which were due to start in Italy in two week's time. My second game was against Spain at Wembley the following March. I played alongside Russell at the back and we took the blame for a 2–1 defeat. Russell was picked again, but I seemed to be out in the wilderness. When the nose injury came only months before the World Cup I didn't think I would have time to stake a claim for a place in the squad.

Out of the blue I was given a chance. I played against Wales at Cardiff and once again I was marking Ian Rush. I did quite well and we won by the only goal. The following month I was substitute for the friendly against Holland and Steve Foster, who was with Brighton at the time, played alongside Phil Thompson at the back. England won 2–0, but I found myself back in the team four days later for the annual clash against Scotland at Hampden.

The England team were staying at Troon, and on the Thursday before the game a group of us, including Russell, Trevor Francis, Viv Anderson, Trevor Brooking and Dave Watson, went into Glasgow to see the Rolling Stones at the Apollo.

Trevor Francis arranged for us to go backstage to meet the Stones before the concert. You can imagine what a thrill it was for me to meet Mick Jagger and Keith Richards. Bill Wyman was very chatty and Charlie Watts kept wishing us the best of luck for the game against Scotland. About ten minutes before the concert started we went out to our seats and were immediately recognized by the Glasgow crowd, who burst into spontaneous Scotland chants and a few anti-England songs until Keith Richards played the first few chords of 'Under My Thumb' and the whole place erupted.

My next drive into Glasgow was nowhere near as relaxed. Scotland versus England is one of the biggest games in the world and means almost as much to players south of the border as it does to the Scots. I also knew that I had to do well for

Alive and kicking! The relief and jubilation after beating Poland in the 1986 World Cup Finals to ensure our place in the second round after being written off by our critics.

Cowboy hats were all the rage when I was a youngster…

…but it's easy to see why I never made the grade as a cricketer.

Lowestoft Grammar School Under-14 football team. That's me in the goalkeeper's jersey.

With Bobby Robson and Bobby
Ferguson – the men who made me
the player I am today.

Riding high with Ipswich. That's me
out-jumping team mate Steve
McCall and Sunderland's Rob
Hindmarch in the 1981–82 season
when we finished second in the First
Division.

My first taste of success. Hugging the UEFA Cup on our open-top bus ride through Ipswich after beating AZ Alkmaar in the final in 1981.

'The best team in Europe.' Back row (*left to right*): Bobby Robson (manager), John Wark, Russell Osman, Paul Cooper, Terry Butcher, Arnold Muhren, Steve McCall, Bobby Ferguson (coach). Front row: Frans Thijssen, Eric Gates, Mick Mills, Paul Mariner, Alan Brazil.

Frank Worthington was always ready to share a laugh and a joke on the pitch. The itinerent forward, seen here in his Birmingham City days, deserved to win more caps for England.

Luton, January 1982. The nightmare began with the broken nose that nearly cost me my life. As the blood streams out, referee Clive Thomas urges me to leave the pitch.

England v. France in the 1982 World Cup. Phil Thompson gives me a lift to out-jump Bossis and Soler (20) during our 3–1 victory.

Yet another England cap! Manager Ron Greenwood handed out the honours at our 1982 World Cup training camp in Bilbao. (*Left to right*): Trevor Brooking, Terry Butcher, Don Howe, Geoff Hurst, Tony Woodcock, Glenn Hoddle, Ron Greenwood, Steve Foster, Kenny Sansom, Graham Rix, Peter Shilton and Viv Anderson.

Ipswich team-mate Paul Mariner and I come to grips with Spain's Santillana during the goalless draw in Madrid. The result meant England went out of the 1982 World Cup even though we were unbeaten.

On tour with England in Sydney, Australia. Russell Osman and I always like to see the local sights.

Our first son Christopher was three months old when he made his début on the terraces for England's game against Kuwait in the 1982 World Cup Finals.

myself to boost my chances of going to Spain.

I was so nervous that the game flashed by. I was up against Kenny Dalglish and Joe Jordan. Alan Brazil, my Ipswich team-mate, wore the number eleven shirt and George Burley was at right-back. I had heard so much about the 'Hampden Roar' but we managed to silence it with an early goal and held on to win 1–0. Both Russell and I were in the World Cup forty. That group was split into two and Russell went to Iceland with the B squad while I was substitute for the senior squad's final preparation game against Finland. I just hoped that I done enough to impress the manager.

Ron Greenwood took a lot of criticism for constantly chang-ing the team, with myself, Alvin Martin and Steve Foster all having games at centre-half in the build up. But the changes gave me the chance to show exactly what I could do. Without the boss's open mind I doubt if I would have been on the plane to Spain.

With only four caps I was a relative newcomer to the England squad and even missed the recording of the World Cup record. I roomed with Peter Withe, who I already knew to be quite a character from our encounters on the pitch. He was an amazing hoarder and our room soon became stock-piled with old newspapers, books, sweets and a variety of soaps among other things. It was like a corner shop, whatever the other lads wanted they would come and ask Withey and he'd be sure to have it somewhere.

We were based in Bilbao, in the heart of the Basque region, where separatists want an independent homeland. There had been a series of bombings in support of their campaign and there was strict security around our hotel. The guards seemed tense, but the atmosphere within the squad was remarkably relaxed. We took over the hotel and before long a games room was established, with pool tables, space invaders and a table-tennis table.

Footballers seem to be competitive whatever they do and there were some fierce contests in the pool championship. We had some handy players like Terry McDermott and Glenn Hoddle, who were like a couple of hustlers. I was quite an ordinary player but I was so determined to improve I used to practice when everyone else was in bed.

Bryan Robson was the Pacman champion. He spent so much time on the machine that the controls gave him blisters on his hands and he needed plasters from the team doctor.

Viv Anderson and Paul Mariner were the table tennis champions and virtually the whole of Bilbao would know if Paul had won a game – he has a very loud voice and greeted each victory with an enormous cheer.

Training was short and sharp and I felt a marked improvement in my game from playing with such good team-mates. Don Howe and Ron Greenwood had done their homework. We knew there would be a lot of movement from opposing forwards, hoping to drag our central defenders apart and we worked hard on countering this in training with plenty of possession play. Don Howe drilled it into us that we had to keep talking to each other and telling team-mates what was going on.

Phil Thompson was an ideal partner for that. Like most Liverpool players he's very vociferous and never stopped talking. On the pitch Phil was the dominant man at the back. He has an incredible will to win, could read the game well, was aggressive in the tackle and always looked comfortable on the ball. He helped me through the early games. After playing alongside Russell for so long at Ipswich I had to adjust to a new partner but Phil made it easy. Off the pitch Phil was a great character. He spent so much time on the phone to his wife that he became known as Busby, after the bird in the British Telecom adverts.

During our first week in Spain the weather had been hot and sticky with a fair sprinkling of refreshing rain. For our first game against France it was brilliant sunshine and stifling heat, with the temperature more than 100° Fahrenheit. I'd been told a couple of days before the game that I would be playing and we had seen several videos of the French team so we knew something about their strengths and weaknesses. Ron Greenwood said to me: 'Go out and win the ball and give it to Bryan Robson or Ray Wilkins.' It sounded simple but my stomach was turning over with the nervous tension and the heat.

The atmosphere was tremendous. There were Union Jacks everywhere as well as thousands of French fans chanting 'Allez la France' which filled the stadium with noise. Within twenty-seven seconds of the start they were silent and we were 1–0 up. Steve Coppell won a throw in near the corner flag on the right. It was early but I decided to go up to the near post. Steve's long throw found me, I back headed across the goal and it fell perfectly for Bryan Robson to hook home unchallenged.

We had practised the move in training but only from the left where Kenny Sansom had a longer throw than Steve. Bryan Robson received a gold watch for the quickest goal ever scored in the World Cup Finals. Steve and I tried to persuade him that he should at least let us have the strap for our part in the build up, but he wouldn't have any of it.

The goal settled my nerves and it took France a while to come back into the game, but after they equalized in the twenty-fifth minute, they finished the first half strongly. Giresse split our defence with a long diagonal ball. I should have played Soler off-side and then as he raced on to the pass, I delayed my challenge only to see him shoot first time past Peter Shilton. I had been caught by the speed of the attack, a harsh lesson in the difference between club and international football. We went in level at half-time and after salt tablets, cold drinks and a freezing cold shower, we came out convinced that our stamina and spirit would see us through.

Half of the pitch was in the shade of the stand and luckily it was down my side during the second half so I managed to stay in the cool for the rest of the game. We regained our composure and goals from Bryan Robson and Paul Mariner gave us a 3–1 victory.

The atmosphere in the dressing room was fantastic. Our campaign had got off to a dream start and it was a marvellous coach journey back to our hotel, cheered all the way as we passed the jubilant England fans.

The next day I was given a stern lecture by Ron Greenwood after being booked for a wild tackle on Rocheteau. It had stemmed from frustration, but the boss was angry that I had lost my head. One more foul and I could have been off leaving us with ten men and putting the game, and our future in the competition, in jeopardy.

It was cooler for our next game against Czechoslovakia who had been held to a draw by Kuwait in their first match. We were unchanged and brimming with confidence after beating France. Our goals came in the second half. Trevor Francis scored the first after their keeper dropped a corner and the second came when the Czech defender Barmos turned a Paul Mariner cross into his own goal. A comfortable 2–0 win and we had created more chances and outplayed the Czechs throughout. More importantly, with two wins out of two games, we had qualified for the second phase.

After another jubilant drive back to the hotel Ron Greenwood let everyone else off the coach until there were only the players, himself and Don Howe left. We wondered what he wanted as it was unusual for him to call such an impromptu meeting. 'Right, lads,' he said. 'I've only got one thing to say to you. Go and get drunk tonight.' They probably heard our cheer in Madrid!

We had worked so hard and were on such a high. There had been so much tension and pressure over the previous weeks and now we had qualified for the next phase we needed a release. No one was going to go crazy, but a party was the ideal way to let off steam.

I had felt more confident against Czechoslovakia. Against France I was so determined to win the ball that I was committing fouls and giving away free-kicks far too often. It was inexperience. I adjusted my game against the Czechs and, as my confidence grew, I felt more comfortable on the ball.

My booking against France meant that I would face an automatic ban if I was cautioned again. The boss left me out of the final group one game against Kuwait to make sure that I would be available for the second phase. I wanted to play but accepted his decision.

Some of the players' wives had already flown out, and Rita came out with Christopher, who was only twelve weeks old, a few days before the game against Kuwait. We couldn't find a babysitter so Christopher came to the match and saw his first World Cup game at the tender age of three months. As I wasn't playing I went and joined them in the stand and spent the second half way up behind the goal feeding Christopher.

A 1–0 victory meant we had won three out of three in the first round. The team was looking good. In goal Peter Shilton had been given the nod over Ray Clemence, after sharing the job in alternate games for more than three years. Mick Mills, my Ipswich team-mate, was right-back and captain. He's a smashing chap and it was reassuring for me to have a familiar face alongside helping me through the game. Steve Foster took my place for the game against Kuwait and with Phil Thompson in the middle and Kenny Sansom at left-back we had a solid defence which conceded one goal in five games in Spain.

Kenny had developed a good understanding with Graham Rix at Arsenal and they carried this through to the England team with Graham operating on the left of midfield flanking the Manchester United pair Bryan Robson and Ray Wilkins. A third United player, Steve Coppell, was a marvellous player to have on the right of midfield, always dangerous going forward and always ready to come back and defend.

Up front Paul Mariner and Trevor Francis had pace and were developing a good understanding. But most attention was focused on two players who weren't in the team. Kevin Keegan and Trevor Brooking, the backbone of the England team for so long, still hadn't taken part in the competition.

Trevor was having trouble with his groin and Kevin was in difficulty with a back injury. We could see there was something seriously wrong when he tried to play a practice match and had to go off. It was obviously something that wouldn't clear up in three or four days and people were worried. Then he disappeared. It was real cloak-and-dagger stuff with him being driven secretly to another airport to avoid the press, and we eventually heard that he had gone to Hamburg for treatment. When he returned he looked a new man.

We were in Madrid for the second phase, in the same group as West Germany and Spain. Once more it was a league rather than a knock-out and we had to play each other once. The top team would go through to the semi-finals and if the teams were level on points the winners would be decided on goal difference.

It was the wrong system for a cup competition and it led to some poor games. In our first match against West Germany neither side could afford to lose, but both were happy to draw and hope that they could beat Spain by the larger margin to go through.

Our tactics against the Germans were criticized for being too negative. But we knew we couldn't afford to pile forward into attack and be caught on the break by a team that had far more international experience than us. The game was dull and I agree with those who say cup football, including the World Cup, should be a straight knock-out competition. It would have meant that both ourselves and West Germany would have had to do something to win the game. In the end they seemed content with a goalless draw and, although Rummenigge hit the bar near the end, neither side looked like scoring.

If anything we had the advantage. The Germans had to play Spain before we did, so we would know what we would have to do to qualify. It had been a disappointing World Cup for the Spaniards, especially in front of their own fans. Their only victory was against Yugoslavia and they finished second in their first round group after drawing with Honduras and losing to Northern Ireland.

Spain continued to disappoint against West Germany and were 2–0 down after seventy-five minutes before Zamora pulled one back nine minutes from time to make the final score 2–1. Nowhere in all of Spain was his goal cheered louder than in the television lounge of our hotel. We now knew we had to win by two clear goals and after beating France and Czechoslovakia by that margin we fancied our chances. Having lost to West Germany, Spain were out of the competition so we knew they would be feeling low.

Steve Coppell was injured, but Ron Greenwood decided against recalling either Keegan or Brooking. They were on the substitutes' bench, with Trevor Francis dropping back to Steve's position and Tony Woodcock coming in up front.

Before the game I saw Uli Stielike, the West German defender, pop into the Spanish dressing room. He played for Real Madrid and obviously knew some of the team and had gone to give them some last minute advice.

There were chances at both ends, and the records show that we had eighteen goal attempts, but the game finished scoreless. Ironically our best chance came to Kevin Keegan shortly after both he and Brooking had come on as substitutes. Trevor sent Bryan Robson clear and his cross found Keegan in front of goal. It was the kind of chance Kevin normally tucks away but this time his header went agonizingly wide.

A few minutes earlier I hit a shot which flashed past the post and, although we kept up the pressure, the goals wouldn't come. We were out of the competition, although we hadn't lost a game. West Germany, who had lost to Algeria in the first round, were through to the semi-finals.

The Germans went on to beat France in a thrilling match, coming back from 3–1 down to win on penalties. The final was an all European affair, as they met Italy. The Italians had started the competition slowly, drawing their first-round games against Poland, Peru and Cameroon before beating the South American challenge of Argentina and Brazil in the second round. Paulo Rossi, the hat-trick hero in the 3–2 win against Brazil, scored both goals in the 2–0 victory over Poland in the semi-final.

The final had a television audience of about one billion around the world. All the goals came in the second half as Rossi, inevitably, Tardelli and Altobelli put Italy three up before Breitner scored a consolation goal for West Germany eight minutes from time.

I had a special interest in Scotland's performances as three Ipswich team-mates were in the squad. George Burley didn't get a game, but John Wark played in all three, scoring twice against New Zealand. Alan Brazil started that game and came on as substitute against the Soviet Union.

Scotland always seem to have a tough draw in the World Cup and 1982 was no exception. They started in the same group as Brazil and the USSR as well as the unfancied New Zealand team, who were their first opponents.

After building up a 3–0 lead by half-time, two moments of madness saw Scotland give away two goals. They went on to win 5–2 but the goals against were to prove expensive.

A few of the England squad leapt out of their chairs as David Narey scored one of the best goals of the tournament to give Scotland the lead against Brazil. But the South Ameicans played their best football of the competition to come back and win 4–1.

Scotland now faced the powerful Soviet side and needed to win to go through. A draw was enough for the USSR; they would finish level on points but the Soviets had a better goal difference. Ironically if Scotland hadn't let in the goals against

New Zealand the goal difference would have been identical and Scotland would go through as higher scorers.

Joe Jordan gave Scotland the lead, Chivadze equalized and then Alan Hansen and Willie Miller got in a muddle to allow Shengelia in to score. Two minutes later Graeme Souness made it 2–2, but there was only six minutes to play and time ran out on the Scots.

On the final whistle, the England squad were out of their chairs again celebrating the demise of the 'auld enemy' – and I'm sure the Scotland lads did the same when we were knocked out.

Obviously I was disappointed for my Ipswich team-mates. It had been a great honour for the club to have six players in the World Cup Finals and showed the depth in quality that we had built up at Portman Road.

8

The International Scene

Most footballers dream about the chance to captain their country, and when Bobby Robson said he wanted me to be skipper when England played Yugoslavia in a European Championship qualifying game at Wembley in November 1986 I was the proudest man in the land. Playing for your country is an honour, to be named as captain is a privilege that I was happy to accept. The roar that greeted us as I led the team on to the pitch sent a tingle down my spine. My mother and father were in the crowd and I knew how much it meant to them. I don't think any of us had expected such a thing to happen ten years previously when I was all set to become a quantity surveyor.

I had captained Ipswich and Rangers before, but I still felt nervous and had to ask Ray Wilkins about the correct protocol for introducing the dignitaries to the players before the game. I also lost the toss, but it didn't matter as we put on a great performance to win 2–0 with goals from Gary Mabutt and Viv Anderson.

My introduction to international football came surprisingly early in my Ipswich career. I had played only eight first team games when I was called into the England Under-21 squad in February 1979. I was the replacement for Sunderland's Shaun Elliott who had withdrawn because of an injury. I was as astonished at my selection as the newspapers seemed to be. We were playing Wales in Swansea and my parents drove down in case I got a game. It poured with rain all night, we won by the only goal but I didn't get on. However, I was thrilled to be part of the set up and having had a taste I wanted some more. It came at the end of the season with a three-game European tour.

We were on tour with the full England team with games against Bulgaria, Sweden and Austria and I was mixing with the big names of the time like Kevin Keegan and Trevor Brooking. It was my first trip into Eastern Europe and I was amazed at how bleak and spartan Bulgaria had been. The hotels were shabby, the beds lumpy, the streets quiet and the city of Sofia was dull and grey.

Dave Sexton was in charge and before the first game against Bulgaria he handed me a pen and some paper. I wasn't playing or even on the subs' bench so he wanted me to sit in the stand and take notes during the game, ticking off the number of times a player touched the ball, which foot they used, how many shots we had on target, how many times we lost possession and so on. I had never come across anything like this before and I was so engrossed in the game that there were times when I forgot to fill in the paper so my records weren't as accurate as they should have been.

A few days later I played my first game for the Under-21 side against Sweden in Vasteras. Our team included several players who went on to win full England caps, including Chris Woods, now a Rangers team-mate of course, Russell Osman, Kenny Sansom and Bryan Robson, who was at West Brom at the time. He scored one of our goals with Cyrille Regis getting the other in a 2–1 win. Playing alongside Russell helped me settle quickly. We had already established a good partnership at Ipswich, and he was an old hand on the international scene having previously played for the England Youth team. The press seemed quite impressed with my performance and I received some good reports.

We were due to fly from Sweden to our next stop in Austria. I was having a laugh and joke with a few reporters at the airport when suddenly a whole crowd closed in on me. One voice said: 'How do you feel about being selected for the England B team against Austria?' I thought they were pulling my leg and said: 'No, I think you've got the wrong person.' Then they showed me the team sheet and sure enough there was my name. I would be playing alongside Billy Wright who was with Everton at the time. It was a marvellous step up for me and an incredible honour after just one full season in the English First Division.

We landed in Austria and faced an arduous five-hour train journey to our venue at Klagenfurt near the border with Yugoslavia. The area was prone to thunderstorms at that time of year and we'd heard reports that a couple of players had been struck by lightning during games earlier that season. It was a terrible night with the atmosphere full of static electricity and we could see a thunderstorm coming towards us. We were leading by a Bryan Robson goal when the storm settled above the pitch. There was torrential rain, thunder and lightning and with an hour of the game gone the referee decided to abandon the match because he thought the conditions were too dangerous. So I only played sixty minutes of B international football but I still received a cap.

It was a great tour and on the long train journey back to Vienna the lads were enjoying themselves with a few beers. Once again Russell decided to play the joker and had brought along some disappearing ink. Joe Corrigan, the former Manchester City goalkeeper was in our compartment and was dressed very smartly in a jacket, white shirt and tie. Russell went straight up to him and squirted the ink all over his shirt. Big Joe looked down in horror as his white shirt turned blue, and gradually his face changed colour as well, to an extremely angry red. I thought he was going to explode when suddenly he ripped off his shirt with buttons flying everywhere, opened the window and threw it out of the train. He pointed at Russell and called him all kinds of names. Russell had been shouting: 'No, Joe, don't do it. Stop, it's a joke! It's disappearing ink!' But Joe had been so angry the shirt was out of the window before he realized what Russell was saying.

Joe was furious. 'Right you lot,' he boomed. 'I want everyone to take off their socks and throw them out the window.' Now Joe is a big and very strong man and not many people argue with him so there was the ridiculous sight of the England football team travelling home in bare feet trying to hide their laughter in case Big Joe took further offence and ordered us to throw even more items of clothing out of the window.

The following season I was a regular in the Under-21 side as we beat Denmark, Bulgaria and Scotland before losing twice in seven days to East Germany in the semi-final of the European Under-21 Championship. In the first leg at Sheffield United's ground, a number of our players were withdrawn from the squad by their clubs and we had a makeshift side. Consequently we played like a team of strangers and lost 2–1. It was an uphill task in the return leg in Jena. I had just broken a bone in my leg which I didn't realize at the time, thinking it was an injury to my calf muscle. But I was determined to play and redeem our earlier performance. After a few minutes the injury was causing me a lot of pain and I had to come off at half-time. We ended up losing 1–0 and going out of the competition.

The Under-21 team is an important stepping stone for future full international players. But the leading clubs in England have so many fixtures, especially if they do well in the cups, that they often have to pull the youngsters out of the squad. Other countries play less league games and will give priority to their international teams. It's something that our authorities have got to sort out. We cannot moan about our comparative lack of international success if we don't allow our international side time to develop.

I have the greatest respect for Ron Greenwood. When I was first called into the England squad he went out of his way to make me feel at ease, and I'm sure that he did the same with all the new players until they settled down. It's a daunting prospect for a young player to be chosen as one of the best twenty-two players in the country. When I arrived I was surrounded by people I considered to be superstars, but Ron treated us all the same and if he saw a player on his own he would go over for a friendly chat to make sure they felt part of the set up. Every time he picked me for the squad he thanked me for coming. It was an honour for me to be included, but I appreciated the boss saying that. He is always the perfect gentleman.

Ron Greenwood is a deep thinker when it comes to football. He has a great love of the game which rubs off on everyone who comes into contact with him. He also understands players. He set up a players' committee to listen to what we had to say and the lads appreciated that. When we stayed at the West Lodge Park Hotel in Cockfosters on the outskirts of north London we usually arrived during the day on Sunday and after a short meeting the evening would be free. Most of us liked to slide off to a pub in Southgate for a couple of pints and catch up on the gossip in other clubs. Ron appreciated that it all helped team spirit. Other managers might disapprove but not Ron. After our meal he would stand up and say: 'Right you lot, isn't it about time you went down the White Hart to pick the team again.'

Ron trusted and respected players so they trusted and respected him. He was savaged by some sections of the press during the World Cup in Spain. There is so much pressure for England to win all the time and every move we, and especially the manager, made was put under a microscope and examined by so-called experts. Ron shielded us from the pressure, but he was treated mercilessly by some reporters. He didn't enjoy press conferences and was more at home communicating with the players than he was with the media. When we were leaving Spain some of the lads spotted a few of the worst offenders in the hotel foyer and told them in no uncertain terms what we thought. There was quite a slanging match and although the lads felt better for getting it off their chests it was an undignified scene and not the Greenwood style at all.

Initially I found it hard to adjust to the international game. It can be physically tough and there is a much greater mental strain on players. If you train properly the physical problems can be overcome, but the game is harder to read and your opponents that much more quick-witted so your reactions have to be swifter in thought and execution. It sharpened me up and made me realize how much room for improvement there was in my game. My faults seemed to be magnified at a higher level. In the First Division I could get away with things like my right foot being weaker than my left and being slow on the turn but I soon found out that it wasn't so easy at international level.

After a game I was mentally exhausted. There are extra pressures before an international anyway and during the game you have to concentrate for the full ninety minutes. One lapse

could cost a goal, but luckily I'm surrounded by players who
keep you on your toes throughout the game. People like Peter
Shilton and Kenny Sansom are always talking about
something, particularly Shilts whose voice invariably has more
exercise than any other part of his body!

I scored my first goal for England against Wales at Wembley
in February 1983 on my twelfth appearance. It was a frosty
night and half the pitch was bone hard while the rest was soft.
The players weren't sure which boots to wear and I settled for
a pair of pimply soles, the sort you wear on Astroturf. I was
marking Ian Rush again. In the first-half a ball broke loose in
our penalty-area and I thought: 'I've got this,' when like
lightning Rushy had nipped in and poked it in the corner. A
few minutes later he hit the post so we could have been two
down instead of just the one goal behind. But I made amends
when I went up for a free-kick and found myself in space with
an open goal and the ball at my feet. I couldn't miss. Later a
Phil Neal penalty gave us a 2–1 victory.

It was early in the Bobby Robson era and since taking over
as manager from Ron Greenwood he had introduced a lot of
new ideas. We were now using Bisham Abbey as our training
centre. For a while we stayed there but, although the sports
facilities are fantastic, the accommodation was a bit like a
university campus and it was agreed that we needed a comfortable hotel where we could relax and rest in peace. More
recently the squad has stayed at a hotel in High Wycombe just
a couple of miles from Bisham Abbey.

In Bobby Robson's early days as England manager he was
very aware of our opponent's strengths. Before our game
against Denmark at Wembley in September 1983 he held a
ninety-minute meeting before the game where he went
through their team talking about their quality in depth. It was
obvious that he was worried about them but he went too far
and his fears rubbed off on the players as we began to think
that we were playing a team of world-beaters. I'm not blaming
the team talk for our 1–0 defeat that night, but at international
level you will always meet quality players. It's important not
to dwell on how marvellous they are but to talk about ways
of beating them. The boss has since learned from that mistake
and his talks are now much more positive which help us get

in the right frame of mind before a game.

The boss is very fond of calling team meetings and at one time the players used to joke about him calling a meeting to decide when to have the next meeting. He is desperate for England to win and feels any bad result far more than the most loyal England supporter. When we lose he sits in the dressing room quietly shaking his head in disbelief. He hardly speaks. I think he regrets that it's not like a club side where he would be able to sort out any problem over the next few days. After an international the players have to leave to rejoin their clubs and he has the frustration of waiting another couple of months before we all get back together again.

Training with England is geared towards helping the players get used to being together again. If we have a game on a Wednesday, we'll normally meet on the Sunday and have just over two days on the training pitch to prepare for the match. Then we may not have another fixture for a couple of months. The manager has to use the limited time available to its maximum and arranges lots of practice games to help us get used to playing alongside each other in match situations. If there are one or two newcomers to the squad it's important for them to know the way England play.

Don Howe generally takes the first part of training with a twenty-minute warm up involving stretching exercises, a bit of running and some ball work. Don is an excellent coach. At some clubs training can be repetitive and boring but Don always prepares different routines to keep the players interested. He likes to introduce competitions, which add an element of fun. We'll have shuttle runs and plenty of games involving the ball. The one I dread is dribbling in and out of cones. Players like Glenn Hoddle and Ray Wilkins are so gifted that they glide through at speed. Alvin Martin and Terry Fenwick have a lot of skill, but I always manage to trip over the ball and it's the one exercise guaranteed to make me look clumsy.

The England set up is also keen on what they call one-on-ones. Ten forwards line-up with a ball each across the half-way line. The defenders start on the edge of the penalty-area and each forward has to try and beat his defender. To add a bit of spice we reverse it after a while and see how good the forwards are at defending and how good the defenders are at taking on their man and scoring.

Training is obviously different at club level. When I was at Ipswich, Fergie would study our opponents and if he spotted a weakness we would concentrate on exploiting that in practice games. And he would also try and iron out our own weaknesses. For example, if he thought we hadn't won the ball well enough in our penalty-area he would play seven or eight forwards against four defenders and see if we could prevent the attackers from scoring.

Most of the stamina work is done with the clubs and that is concentrated mainly during the pre-season. It was particularly hard at Ipswich. We trained at the Martlesham Police head-quarters, which is a lovely setting in the heart of Suffolk. In mid-July it was always hot. The training was hard enough, the heat made it unbearable at times.

I was lucky because I would stay fit through being away on tour with England during the close season. I would have a lay off of about four weeks which was enough time for my body to rest without losing my fitness. Other lads would have eight weeks off and come back with beer bellies and more than a few extra pounds. After the 1982 World Cup I had less than two weeks between returning from Spain and the start of pre-season training. It's important for players to have some kind of break because we are pushing our bodies to the limit for so much of the year that there's a danger we can push too far.

Pre-season training involves a lot of running which is why footballers generally detest it. One much feared exercise at Ipswich involved five laps of the athletics track, with a time limit of one and a half minutes for each lap. Then after a short rest you had to run four laps, then three, two and then one. I'm quite good at the longer distances, but in the shorter runs I would be left way behind people like Michael Cole who's off like an Olympic 400 metre runner. After that we moved to the 'doggy pit' for a series of shuttle runs, again all timed against the clock. The training needs to be hard to carry you through a gruelling season where you'll probably play fifty games or more.

Players always moan about work and complain that they are doing too much, but it's important to put your back into it. Managers aren't stupid and they are aware that if you do too much you can leave all the hard work on the training pitch and not be able to perform in a game. I moan about exercises that drag on and on, for example interminable shooting sessions. Players lose interest and start going through the motions and you don't develop the sharp reactions you would need on match-day. Exercises need to be short and sharp to keep everyone on their toes.

A good session should include a warm-up, perhaps a bit of running such as a few shuttles and a five-a-side which is allowed to flow. Too often because they are controlled with rules such as off-side, one or two touch and without a referee, disputes arise and the game ends up as a farce. Stamina is important but I don't believe in running hard and leaving the ball behind. Players work harder when the ball is involved and Liverpool and Everton seem to have enjoyed their success on a training diet of daily five-a-sides and little else.

I love travelling and I have been lucky that football has taken me all over the world from Australia to Latin America. Unfortunately we don't have as much time as I would like to look around the different places we visit, but I always try to pop out to an art gallery if I can. I love going to the Rijks Museum in Amsterdam, which has paintings by all the great Dutch artists, and when I was in Los Angeles playing for the Rest of the World against the Americas I saw a fascinating exhibition on impressionism. I've been to some great places and once even ended up in a brothel! That was in Paris in February 1984. We had lost 2–0 to France, for whom Michel Platini had once again been superb. He scored twice and there was a buzz of expectancy in the crowd every time he touched the ball. He's been one of the all-time greats and I'm proud to have swapped shirts with him after that game. We had a fair team and I partnered Graham Roberts, who's now at Rangers of course, but France were coming to the boil and went on to win the European Championship that summer.

After the game a few of the lads tried to get in to some of the Paris discos without any success. The doormen thought we were English supporters some of whom had been on the rampage that evening. We tried to convince them that we were in fact the team but my French explanation 'Jouers de football' accompanied by a demonstratation from others kicking imaginary balls wasn't good enough.

We found a taxi-driver who could speak a bit of English and we asked him to take us to a night-club. 'I know a nice one,' he said with a wink and we sped off into the Paris night. We walked into a scene which was like something out of a film. It was a small bar with red lights on low and about a dozen well made up women lounging around. It didn't take long to put two and two together and we thought: 'Bloody hell. What would happen if this got in the papers!' I could imagine the headlines 'England football team in brothel shock' and it added extra poignancy to a familiar chant from the terraces when a player misses an open goal. After a quick drink we left discreetly. I counted all the boys in and I counted them all out again and I can safely say that nothing untoward happened.

In November 1984 we went to Istanbul to play Turkey in a World Cup qualifying game and it's a trip that I will never forget. Before the game the Turks had seemed confident about getting a result and the stadium, which was a bit like an English Third or Fourth Division ground, was packed with 40,000 people all in fine voice creating one of the best atmospheres that I have ever known at a football match. We had expected a tough game but in the tunnel on the way to the pitch we could sense that the Turkish players looked frightened and beaten before we started. We were 3–0 up at half-time and went on to win 8–0, Bryan Robson scoring three, Tony Woodcock and John Barnes getting two each and Viv Anderson scoring the other one. We could have had more and the fans were tremendous after the game giving us a fantastic reception as they applauded us off the pitch.

One of the waiters from a hotel we used with Ipswich was Turkish and was back in Istanbul. While we were there he took us around the sights including the amazing grand bazaar. As soon as people saw that we were westerners they flocked around us trying to sell anything from Turkish carpets to Turkish coffee.

When you travel with England one of the main problems is having so much spare time on your hands with so little to do. We stay in hotels and after training we have the rest of the day to ourselves. It's not always possible to go sightseeing and quite often we are advised to rest. There is a thriving card school, although I am not a member. I can't afford it and prefer to gamble during a day at the races. In my early England days a group of us would go greyhound racing at Wembley Stadium on Monday nights. Terry McDermott, Mick Mills, Paul Mariner, Trevor Brooking and myself became regulars. I didn't win much but it was always a good night out and strange to see Wembley in a different light.

In 1985 we went to Mexico City for a three-game tour to acclimatize ourselves to playing at altitude before the World Cup Finals twelve months later. It was a superb idea and we soon found how breathless you become when you run at altitude. I felt as though my lungs were on fire. We also discovered that the effects of alcohol are even worse when you are high up. We really suffered during a training session after a couple of beers the night before. The doctors had warned us that it would affect us and it was an important lesson. The following year during the World Cup Finals the lads introduced a voluntary ban on alcohol. Some of the papers were surprised that we didn't drink when we were in Colorado, but our minds were attuned to the job ahead. There was a feeling that if our bodies were right then other things should fall into place.

While we were in Mexico in 1985 we settled down in our hotel TV lounge to watch Liverpool play Juventus in the European Cup Final. The match was supposed to be live and when the screen remained blank I went back to my room to phone Rita and ask her the latest score. I was horrified when she told me about the terrible fights that had gone on and how a wall had collapsed and more than thirty people had died. The entire England squad felt numb. The game we loved was being destroyed by hooligans and there was nothing we could do.

Hooliganism has haunted English football for too long. I have witnessed scenes in Paris where fans ran amok and started fights on the terraces while we were warming up for the game. I don't understand why they do it. They are not interested in the game they just go along to cause trouble. Perhaps stiffer penalties will act as a deterrent, and if England fans cause trouble abroad then take away their passports. Unfortunately, I don't think either of those measures will be enough. Football is the focal point for the hooligans but violence is a social disease.

I think every footballer would like to see an end to racist chanting from the terraces. It's not clever and it certainly isn't funny. When I go away with the England team I room with a black player and I have become more aware of racist chants. On one England tour a handful of National Front members were shouting racist remarks at the black players in the squad and I'm delighted to say that the white lads in the team were quick to react and sort out the loudmouths.

The only England tour that I didn't enjoy was to Australia in June 1983. It was the end of a long, hard season with Ipswich and a demanding trip down under, where soccer is a minority sport behind cricket, rugby and Australian rules football, was the last thing I needed. Our first game was at the Sydney cricket ground. The pitch was rock hard and the cricket square stuck out like a lump more than a foot higher than the rest of the pitch. Australia put ten men behind the ball and the game was a drab 0–0 draw. We scrambled a 1–0 win in Brisbane, and in the third game in Melbourne Trevor Francis scored to give us the lead before they equalized with what seemed to be their one and only attack of the tour. The trip was a nightmare and I couldn't wait to get home.

One of the best places to play is Scandinavia where the people are friendly, the food is always good and the accommodation is excellent. By contrast our trip to Tbilisi to play the Soviet Union was awful. Our rooms were dirty, the sheets looked as though they had never been washed and my room-mate, Alvin Martin, and I wore our training kit in bed to protect us from lice and bugs. The towels were tiny moth-eaten things which had no chance of drying anybody. The food was terrible and the lights were on such a low wattage that it was impossible to read.

Alvin and I went for a walk in the evening and were amazed at how quiet the streets were. It was like a ghost town and you could sense the feeling that 'Big Brother' was watching you.

Alvin is a great character and has one of those faces that seems to attract pests. If ever anyone wants to hassle us they always make for Alvin. He is such a nice man that he always takes time to talk to them and in Tbilisi the locals were surrounding him offering to change money and one of them wanted to buy his trousers.

People always speculate about the best partnership at the heart of the England defence. I have partnered Russell, Alvin, Mark Wright, Terry Fenwick and Graham Roberts who have all been in for a few games, but because of injuries, suspensions or club commitments, no one has had a really long run. I have been the lucky one who has kept a regular place.

Mark Wright is quick and reads the game well. He was unlucky to break a leg and miss the World Cup in Mexico where I think he would have done well. Arsenal's Tony Adams is another fine defender. He played his first full international against Spain in Madrid when he was 20 but he already seemed remarkably mature. He's strong, cool and knocks the ball around well. He certainly wasn't overawed on his England debut. He kept talking all the game and didn't mince words when he wanted to tell someone that they were out of position. He settled into the squad very quickly and I think it helped him to have his Arsenal colleagues Viv Anderson and Kenny Sansom alongside him during the game and Don Howe, his former manager, shouting advice. The Arsenal lads have nick-named him 'Rodders' after the TV character in 'Only Fools and Horses' but Tony doesn't seem to mind. Our first game together was against Spain and afterwards he came up to me and said how much he had enjoyed playing alongside me which was a smashing thing to say.

The England defence is often criticised in the newspapers but our record is good and the critics are often unfair. In 14 games in 1986 we conceded only six goals and before then you had to go back to 1979 to find the last time that we conceded more than two goals in one game.

England's home games are, of course, played at Wembley and I used to think it was heresy to suggest playing them anywhere else. It is still a fantastic stadium and everyone dreams of playing there, but it has such a reputation world-wide that it also brings out the best in players from other countries as well. Perhaps it would be a good idea for us to play internationals at other grounds around the country. If we played at Anfield or Old Trafford, for example, with the fans close to the pitch and making a lot of noise from the start it would intimidate our opponents and give us an advantage. It's something that other countries use when they play us and it can have an effect on the way a team play.

The England players are paid £100 in appearance money with a bonus if we win. The basic money is much less than other internationals in Europe who receive between £2,000 and £3,000 a game. Perhaps we don't receive the going rate, but I would play for England for nothing because the honour means so much to me and I am sure that the other players feel the same way. It's a fantastic feeling when you pull that white shirt on and I feel as proud now as I did on my first appearance.

9

Hard Times at Portman Road

As my own career went from strength to strength the fortunes of Ipswich Town started to decline. From championship contenders each season we became involved in an annual battle to avoid relegation. Twice we avoided the drop thanks to marvellous end of season recoveries and we looked to have done enough to stay up at the end of the 1985–6 season, but our poor goal-scoring – thirty-two goals in forty two games – and two defeats in our last two games meant that we went down with West Brom and Birmingham City.

It wasn't all doom and gloom. We had some good youngsters emerge into the first team and a couple of good cup runs. We were cheated out of a place at Wembley after being kicked off the park by Norwich in the Milk Cup semi-final in 1985 and gave Everton a scare in the quarter-finals of the FA Cup in the same year. But in the end too many experienced players left in too short a time for us to be able to sustain our position at the top of the First Division. Nine internationals left the club in three years and no matter how good the young players coming through may be, you cannot expect them to replace experience of that calibre.

On reflection our problems probably started when Arnold Muhren left in the summer of 1982. His contract had expired after four years with the club and, as he was thirty-one, he wanted to make himself financially secure before he retired. He joined Manchester United and we were all sad to see him go. He had been one of the reasons for our success, but even without Arnold we approached the 1982–83 season with optimism.

Bobby Robson had also left to take over as England manager and he was replaced by Bobby Ferguson, the first team coach. Fergie had often been in charge of the team when Bobby Robson was away watching other players or teams and we knew what he was like. It was a smooth transfer of power in the Liverpool tradition and was better than an outsider coming in and causing upheaval by wanting to change everything. We had a winning formula and although Fergie would have his own ideas about the team it was unlikely that he would radically alter a successful side.

Bobby Robson had been at Ipswich for thirteen years and built us into one of the best teams in the country. In the ten years after 1972, the club won two cups and only once finished outside the top six in the First Division. If the team stayed together, we didn't see why we couldn't do what we had threatened to do for so long and win the League.

We had a terrible start to the new season and after seven games we were bottom of the table still without a win. We recovered in style with a 6–0 win away at Notts County followed by a 1–0 victory over Liverpool at Portman Road, but it was an up and down season and we didn't put together a string of results for any long period of time.

A poor end to the season, with only three wins from our last eleven games saw us finish ninth. Plenty of teams would be happy with that, but after the standard we had set ourselves it was a huge disappointment. To make matters worse we failed to qualify for Europe. We had expected the good times to continue and perhaps there were occasions when we didn't put in the effort, thinking the result would come anyway. But other teams were used to the Ipswich 'system' and were developing ways of combating Eric Gates. Teams who had been frightened of us a year or two earlier were now taking points off us.

We went out of the UEFA Cup in the first round. A 3–0 defeat in the first leg away to Roma before a passionate 60,000 crowd left us a mountain to climb. In the second leg Eric Gates put us 1–0 up and then an own goal put us 3–2 behind on aggregate shortly after half-time. For a while it looked as though we could do it, but Roma pulled one back, Maldera hitting a tremendous free-kick into the top corner. It was a marvellous goal and gave Laurie Sivell, our keeper, no chance. I scored to make it 3–1 on the night but we needed another two to go through because of the away goals rule. We tried and tried but it wouldn't come.

In the domestic cup competitions we always seemed to be drawn against either Liverpool, Shrewsbury or Norwich. Liverpool knocked us out of the Milk Cup at the first hurdle, beating us 2–1 in the first leg at Portman Road and 2–0 at Anfield. We were terrible and gave up without a fight. After the game Bobby Ferguson called a meeting at our Haydock hotel to sort out what was going wrong.

The hotel produced a crate of beer and everyone was supposed to say their piece. Whoever was in charge of the beer ordered Carlsberg Special Brew, which is a bit like rocket fuel. After a couple of these we were well away and the best of friends again. Four days later we beat West Brom 6–1 and had a brief revival, but we couldn't get a good run going.

In the FA Cup we beat Charlton in the third round coming back from 2–0 down to win 3–2. They had Allan Simmonsen in their team and although the pitch was sticky and heavy and unsuitable for a slight player like him he still impressed us all.

After beating Grimsby in the fourth round we went to Norwich in the fifth. I still have nightmares about that game now as it was my mistake that set up the only goal. The game was only five minutes old when a long ball was played up towards Keith Bertschin, the Norwich centre-forward. I tried to get in front of him to cut the pass out but completely misread the bounce. The ball went right over my foot leaving Bertschin free to run through unchallenged and score. It was a stupid mistake and Fergie gave me so much stick after the game.

The following season, 1983–4, we lost to Norwich again, this time in the fourth round of the Milk Cup at Portman Road. It was our worst display for years. The night before the game, Sadie, our labrador, had given birth to nine puppies. I had stayed up to make sure she was all right. It was a marvellous experience to watch these nine little creatures come into the world and I wanted to make sure Sadie didn't roll over and squash any. I thought it was a good omen but Mick Channon scored the only goal to see Norwich through.

The team that had been so successful was already starting to break up. As well as Arnold, three other players had left during the previous season. Mick Mills went to Southampton, Alan Brazil to Spurs and Frans Thijssen to Vancouver White-caps. We weren't surprised when Alan left as we had sensed that he and Fergie had their differences, but he had left a huge gap up front. He had scored eighty goals in 195 games for the club and would be hard to replace.

Mick Mills had been in the Ipswich team when I first came to Portman Road as a schoolboy to stand on the terraces. He was an inspirational figure, who as captain, had always led by example. He was marvellous to play alongside and was never flustered no matter how tough the going.

Arnold and Frans had made us tick with their continental approach to the game. To lose two world class players in such a short time would be a blow for any team.

By the end of the 1983–4 season two more internationals had left. Both Paul Mariner and John Wark asked for transfers and left for Arsenal and Liverpool respectively. Both had given Ipswich good service, but they wanted to get away for their own reasons. The fans turned on them and when they came back with their new clubs they were jeered.

I can understand the disappointment of the supporters when they see good players leave, but footballers have a short life. It may sound brutal, but you have to earn as much money as you can when you are at your peak because you don't stay at the top for long. If a bank clerk or a bricklayer changes jobs because they want more money or a new challenge then people respect them for it. If a footballer does the same people accuse them of being greedy.

The rest of the team were sad to see so many players go. It obviously unsettled the team but in another way it helped pull us together as we knew that even more was expected from us.

Russell Osman took over as captain from Paul Mariner and in his first game was sent off as we lost 3–2 at Southampton. He was suspended and Fergie asked me to be captain for the next game against Arsenal. I was thrilled. It had been an ambition since I was at school and I said yes immediately in case he changed his mind.

It was a tremendous honour and to me the job meant more than just tossing the coin at the start of the game.

It was a difficult time for the club. Key players had left and young players coming into the side needed encouragement.

Our form took a tumble and we had a grim fight against relegation. Our trouble started on 2 January 1984 when we lost 2–1 away to West Brom. It was the start of a terrible run where we lost ten of our next eleven League games, crashed out of the FA Cup at Shrewsbury and became everyone's favourites for relegation. Our misery continued until the end of March when we gained a 0–0 draw at home to Watford. They had a chance near the end to give them the game but missed it and let us off the hook. We were in the bottom three at the time and that point, our first in eight games, was the start of our recovery. However, while on international duty I strained the ligaments in my left knee playing for England against Northern Ireland at Wembley. I struggled to get fit for the game at home to Nottingham Forest ten days later only to strain the ligament in my other knee and finish the game in agony. Mich D'Avray scored with a looping header to give us a point from a 2–2 draw which made me feel better, but as soon as I saw a specialist he told me that I would be out for the rest of the season. George Burley was carried off in the same game with cartilage problems and also missed the rest of the season.

With six games to play we were twentieth, four points behind the team in nineteenth position, and the bookmakers made us favourite to go down. So many players had left and, now George and I were injured, Bobby Ferguson was forced to introduce youngsters into the team. Players like Mark Brennan, Ian Cranson and Frank Yallop were thrown in at the deep end. Ideally you don't introduce young, inexperienced players to a struggling side but we had no choice and they responded superbly.

We beat Wolves and Norwich and drew 2–2 at Liverpool. I listened to that game on the radio and went berserk when Gatesy scored the equalizer. They were the champions that season and the point at Anfield had been a fantastic achievement.

We had a 1–0 victory over Sunderland at home and faced a difficult trip to Manchester United before our last game at home to Villa. I couldn't face another ninety minutes of radio commentary. I had to see what was happening for myself in such an important game so I went up to Old Trafford with Rita and Russell's girl friend Louise.

Sitting in the stand was harder than playing and in my mind I kicked every ball as we came back from a goal down to win 2–1. It meant we were safe. Russell had been superb and his spirit and determination had been a perfect example to the younger players.

We beat Villa in our last game and finished twelfth thanks to that run of five wins in our last seven games. Notts County and Wolves went down along with Birmingham City, but we knew it had been close. Five points separated the nine teams fighting to avoid the third relegation spot and although twelfth sounded respectable we were only five points away from Division Two.

My knee was still sore and I had to pull out of the England summer tour to South America. I missed the games in Brazil, Uruguay and Chile and watched on TV as John Barnes scored that incredible goal in Rio de Janeiro and Mark Hateley made an international name for himself.

At least I could spend some time in Ipswich with Rita. That summer I went into Portman Road nearly every day for extra training to try and build the knee up in time for the next season. We had a new kit, modelled on that worn by the French team which won the European Championships in such style that June. Unfortunately once the season began we didn't play as well as they had and once again found ourselves at the wrong end of the table. Between October and January we had another terrible run losing nine League games out of eleven.

Once a side slips into a run like that you think it's never going to end. No matter how we changed the side we kept giving away silly goals, and where a few years earlier we didn't believe that we could ever lose now we were wondering when our next victory was going to be. Confidence drained away and as soon as we conceded a goal you knew what was going through people's minds 'Oh no, here we go again.'

We seemed to save our best performances for the cups and

deserved to be at Wembley for the final of the Milk Cup in the
1984–85 season. Victories over Derby, Newcastle, Oxford and
QPR had seen us through to the semi-final where we were
drawn against Norwich.

Bad weather delayed the first leg at Portman Road until the
end of February. Another big crowd turned up to see us win
1–0, Mich D'Avray scoring the only goal. Chris Woods, now
a team-mate at Rangers, was in goal for Norwich that day and
pulled off some marvellous saves to keep our lead down to a
single goal.

The second leg at Norwich was a nasty affair. Mich D'Avray
went off with a broken nose after seventeen minutes following
an accidental clash of heads with Dave Watson, the Norwich
centre-half.

John Deehan scored to put Norwich level on aggregate by
half-time, but there were a couple of Norwich players who
seemed more intent on kicking the man rather than the ball.
The referee, Keith Hackett, appeared to be determined to keep
the game flowing and let some outrageous tackles go unpunished, especially one late challenge on Steve McCall. We had
already used our substitute and Steve was reduced to a pass-
enger for the last hour of the game.

We had tried to play constructive football, but some of our
players had been intimidated by a few of the tackles. Four
minutes from time Steve Bruce headed Norwich's second goal
from a Mark Barham corner to put them through to Wembley.
I was devastated. I couldn't believe that we had allowed ourselves to be kicked out of the cup. I stormed into the changing
room and kicked a hole in the door, an action I regretted
afterwards as I should have shown that sort of aggression on
the pitch. I was still angry when I left for home and drove the
entire journey on the wrong side of the road. I was so mad I
didn't care what happened to me. To be so close to Wembley
and lose like that, especially to Norwich, hurt me deeply.

I think Bobby Ferguson made one important mistake. He left
out Russell Osman when we needed his experience, aggression
and determination. It was frustrating for me to know that
Russell, with all his fighting qualities, was watching from the
stand when he should have been on the pitch.

We had another good run in the FA Cup beating Bristol

Rovers and Gillingham before winning a tremendous fifth-round tie against Sheffield Wednesday 3–2. In the sixth round we were away to the Cup-holders Everton. Goals from Kevin Wilson and Romeo Zondervan gave us a 2–1 lead which we held until the last few minutes when Derek Mountfield scored their equalizer after Steve McCall had been sent off.

Nearly 28,000 fans turned up at Portman Road for the replay and it was just like the old days with a packed ground and a great atmosphere. But this time we found Everton harder to break down and they won by the only goal of the game, a penalty from Graham Sharp. It was a harsh decision. The pitch was hard and the ball bounced up and hit Russell on the arm. It was obvious to everyone, except the referee, that it was accidental.

Everton went on to lose to Manchester United in the final but they had the consolation of winning the League, finishing thirteen points ahead of Liverpool in second place. We had gone out of two cups in less than a week and now faced a grim battle against relegation for the rest of the season.

Almost inevitably there was a reaction and three days after losing to Everton we lost 3–0 to QPR at Loftus Road, our tenth League defeat in thirteen games. We picked up draws against Arsenal and at home to Newcastle, but things reached rock bottom when we lost 3–1 away to Luton at the end of March.

Both Paul Cooper and I had made mistakes which cost us the game. Our position was looking precarious and team spirit was fading. Like most sides which go through a bad run, cliques formed which would look for people to blame for the lack of success. It was starting to lead to some bad feeling in the changing room so we decided to so something about it. On the coach journey back from Luton, Fergie spent an hour running through our faults. Normally players would drift off home when we arrived back at Ipswich but that night eight of us went off to the pub to talk about the manager's comments.

It was something we hadn't done for a long time and there were players who never socialized together sitting in the Ipswich Arms getting stuck into a few pints. It seemed to clear the air. We agreed that individual mistakes had cost us games but decided it was no use blaming people all the time, instead we should stick together as a team. I think we were all drunk when we eventually left the pub, but it had been a great night and marked the start of our recovery.

We won our next three games beating West Brom, Forest and Norwich. That 2–0 victory at Carrow Road gave us the most satisfaction. Norwich had just beaten Sunderland in the Milk Cup Final and were on a high. I noticed that they had put a new door on the visitors changing room after our semi-final. I was still angry about that game and there was no way I was going to lose this one.

Norwich seemed to think that they were on to three easy points, but we played well and surprised them. I scored in the first half and set up a second for Mich D'Avray as we coasted to a 2–0 victory. We went on to beat Tottenham, earning the Fiat team performance of the week award, and Leicester, and drew with Liverpool. Further wins against Stoke and Sunderland meant we stayed up and, ironically, Norwich, who had appeared to be safe in mid-table a few weeks earlier, found themselves relegated.

The season had finished well for us and I went off to Mexico with the England team for a three-week tour to acclimatize ourselves for the World Cup finals the following year. I came back raring to go but once again an injury put me out of the game for a couple of months.

I picked the injury up in a pre-season friendly. A sign of the times perhaps that whereas a few seasons ago Ipswich would go to places like Canada or Hawaii this year we toured the midlands with games against Burton Albion, Nuneaton and Notts County.

This time I had cartilage trouble. Against Notts County I went to block a cross and the ball hit me on the toes twisting my knee. I felt it but it didn't seem serious at the time. When I trained the following week the knee started to swell and became so big that I couldn't run. The club surgeon, Andrew Gibb, had a look and told me I had torn a cartilage and that I would be out for four weeks missing the start of the season.

We had a hard opening programme and lost three of the first five games. Russell had been transferred to Leicester and Eric Gates had gone to Sunderland, so only three of the UEFA Cup-winning side were still at the club – Paul Cooper, Steve McCall and myself.

It was sad to see Russell go. We had come through so much together and thought we would play out our careers alongside each other. Both Bobby Robson and Bobby Ferguson had said they would build a team around us. But Russell had been unhappy for the last year and felt the time was right for a move. Ipswich's loss has since been Leicester's gain.

I was desperate to play again. I'm normally a quick healer and at the beginning of September I felt good enough in training to return to the first team for the game at West Brom. Looking back, I probably came back too soon. I wasn't fully fit and by the end of my game my right calf had swollen so much it was twice the size of my left one. I had played without too much pain and we had won 2–1, so I was quite pleased with the day's work.

The swelling wouldn't go down. In fact, my knee blew up so much that I could hardly bend it. I had to withdraw from the England squad to play Romania and was told to stay at home and rest. It seemed to get worse and when the surgeons eventually looked they found another piece of torn cartilage which meant a second operation.

After another two months of frustration, waiting for the knee to heal and then slowly getting back into full training, I made my second come back in the middle of November at home to Everton. That was quite a game. We were one off the bottom and they were chasing the title once more, but we were 2–0 up early on and playing well. Then just before half-time the ball dropped perfectly for Adrian Heath to score and make it 2–1.

In the second half they came out with new confidence while we were a bit tentative after conceding a goal. They scored twice through Sharp and Sheedy and then I scored to make it 3–3. The game was in the melting pot when we had what we thought was a goal disallowed. Almost from the break out of defence Everton were awarded a penalty which Trevor Steven scored to make it 4–3.

It was an incredible match which we should have won. Even the Everton bench didn't know why our 'goal' was disallowed.

We were in another seven goal thriller the following week at Oxford. We went 3–0 up shortly after half-time and looked to be heading for a good away win when they came back, scored four and stole the game. It was the first time I had ever lost a three-goal lead. Bobby Ferguson didn't know what to say. He walked in to the changing rooms five minutes before the end. Oxford had just scored their fourth and he couldn't bear to watch any more. It was disgraceful from our point of view. Most of the goals came from crosses. One hit John Aldridge on the knee and went in and it was like a nightmare where we had no control over what was happening to us.

It was a terrible journey home. We had scored six goals in two games and had nothing to show for it. That was especially ironic when you consider that we only scored thirty-two goals all season. In the New Year our form improved and we climbed out of the bottom three.

We came back from a goal behind to beat Liverpool at home and thought that at last we had turned the corner. Then the bad weather took hold and we didn't have another League game for four weeks.

We beat Nottingham Forest 1–0, but then we lost games we should have won away to Arsenal and at home to Newcastle. We lost 2–0 at home to Leicester, which sent Russell home happy, but was a terrible result for us. If we had beaten them it would have lifted us up the table and pushed them further into trouble. Instead they leapfrogged over us and we slipped into the relegation zone once more.

One of the best games of the season was the return match against Oxford. They had just won the Milk Cup but needed the points to avoid relegation. We had to win. It was our last home game and we needed the points to have a chance of staying up.

At half-time Oxford were one up thanks to a goal from John Aldridge. We had been nervous and hesitant and received a roasting from Fergie. But in the second half we settled and found a new determination. Jason Dozell scored to make it 1–1 and a minute later I scored with a right foot volley to put us in the lead.

Ten minutes later I received a nasty cut on my forehead after a collision with Oxford's Trevor Hebberd and had to go off. I was receiving treatment by the side of our goal with my back to the pitch. When our physio, Brian Owen, took the sponge away the first thing I saw was the ball nestled in the corner of our net. Les Phillips had scored for Oxford.

Brian rushed me into the changing rooms to stitch the wound and a few minutes later I came out with headband and bandage, looking like Bill Beaumont. The crowd gave me a tremendous reception and you could sense how much they were willing us to win. We threw everything into attack and in injury time we were awarded a free-kick on the edge of the Oxford penalty-area.

It was our last chance and there is always the danger that someone will panic and waste the opportunity. I made straight for the ball to stop anyone doing anything hasty. I remember telling everyone to stay calm, but I could feel the tension as the referee moved the seven-man Oxford wall back ten yards. Mark Brennan touched the ball to Ian Atkins and his shot took a deflection off Kevin Wilson, who was on the end of the wall. Alan Judge had committed himself and was helpless as the ball rolled over the line.

The crowd went crackers. Hundreds of people invaded the pitch and it was as if we had won the League rather than scraped a late win against another team at the bottom of the table.

We had two more games to play, both away from home, and we needed two points to be sure of staying up. The first, four days later, was at West Ham who were still in with an outside chance of winning the League. More than 31,000, their biggest crowd of the season, squashed into Upton Park. We contained them well and midway through the second-half Kevin Wilson gave us the lead. All we had to do was hold on, but then Alan Dickens miscued a shot which deceived Paul Cooper to make it 1–1.

West Ham seemed to gain renewed hope and threw everything at us, but we were grimly hanging on until two minutes from the end. Mark Ward, the West Ham number seven, took an exaggerated dive in the penalty-area after being tackled by Nigel Gleghorn. It was a fair tackle, Nigel had played the ball and come away with it cleanly. The crowd were shouting for a penalty, as they do in those situations, especially with the time running out. Astonishingly the referee, Gerald Ashby, pointed to the spot.

I was furious. It was obvious to me that the referee had been swayed by the crowd. Ward had dived quite blatantly and once the penalty was given he blew a kiss at Nigel Gleghorn as if to say: 'I've got away with it!' My protests earned me a booking and inevitably Ray Stewart scored West Ham's winner from the penalty-kick.

When the final whistle went I snapped and chased after Mr Ashby to explain my feelings. As far as I was concerned his mistake at an important stage of the game could cost Ipswich Town their place in the First Division. I told him, quite forcibly, what I thought and had to be restrained by a couple of policemen.

Phil Parkes, the West Ham goalkeeper, and Bobby Ferguson tried to drag me away and I ended up accidentally elbowing Fergie in the face.

I know I was wrong and that what I did was inexcusable. People who know me off the pitch see me as a quiet, easy going character and can't understand why I should react like that. But football is an emotional game and you play for high stakes. And in my opinion the tension at the bottom of the table is far higher than anything you feel at the top. If you lose a game there's the prospect of dropping out of the First Division and losing face with your supporters.

There was a big fuss about the whole incident and I was charged with bringing the game into disrepute. There was even talk of the FA stepping in to ban me from the World Cup, but in the end I was fined a thousand pounds and warned as to my future conduct.

Our last game was at Sheffield Wednesday. Thousands of fans made the trip from Suffolk to see if we could perform our annual escape trick again. Some were in fancy dress and they treated the game like a cup final creating a great carnival atmosphere.

We had a couple of chances and would have scored but for some excellent saves from the Wednesday keeper Martin Hodge. I kept thinking, 'Why does he have to choose today to really turn it on?' With fifteen minutes to go Carl Shutt beat me for pace on the wing and whipped in a cross. Brian Marwood just got a toe to it before our defenders and it went in off the bar.

We pressed forward for the rest of the game but couldn't

score. I was in tears at the end and felt so sorry for the fans who had been tremendous throughout the game. Paul Hart, the Wednesday centre-half, shook hands and said how well we had played and that he hoped we stayed up because we were a good footballing side. It was nice of him but I knew deep down that we had lost our chance.

Our fate lay in the hands of Oxford. If they won their last game two days later at home to Arsenal they would stay up and we would go down. In such a game you had to fancy Oxford. They were a fair side and had everything to play for while Arsenal's season had petered out.

Jim Rosenthal, the ITV sports commentator, came round for lunch and to listen to the game on the radio. He's a big Oxford fan and when the score came through 'Oxford 3, Arsenal 0' he was obviously delighted but saddened that a friendly club like Ipswich should go down. I had expected it but I was still very upset.

People say other clubs like Manchester United and Spurs went down, rebuilt successfully and came back with stronger teams. But I believe that if you are ambitious you should stay in the First Division and, if necessary, rebuild there rather than drop down and try and win promotion.

In the end we only had ourselves to blame. We didn't score enough goals –thirty-two in forty-two games – and had lost too many players over the years.

The young players who were in the team had only known a struggling side and the pressures of playing at the wrong end of the table. If you are riding high with a few good wins under your belt the game seems easy and the goals seem to come regularly. But when you are struggling the game seems hard and when there's a chance you tend to think, 'I've got to score', and you end up snatching at a shot and ballooning the ball over the bar when you should hit the target.

We never tried to kick our way out of trouble and always played good attacking football. A lot of people have said to me how sad they were to see Ipswich go down. It's a friendly club and everyone enjoys coming there from players and directors to supporters.

So what went wrong with Ipswich? Why did a club that had been so successful a few years earlier find itself struggling and eventually relegated? Bobby Robson's departure was obviously a major blow. His influence was everywhere and he had been responsible for much more than just team selection.

On the pitch, losing Arnold Muhren was the start of our slide. Like Robson he had become vital to the club's success and he was impossible to replace.

Many supporters blame the new Pioneer Stand which cost £1.5 million – money which some fans feel should have been spent on players. I believe the decision to build the new stand was taken in the best interests of the club. The idea was to provide better facilities for the fans so they could watch a team that was expected to compete with the best in Europe. Nobody could have envisaged the exodus of top players over the next three or four seasons. It's wrong to say that the players were sold purely to pay for the stand. Each one was ambitious and for their own reasons wanted to get away. I was as sad as the supporters were to see them go as they were all good friends as well as good players.

Perhaps the directors were guilty of putting the comfort of the fans ahead of the make-up of the team. If they hadn't spent so much on the stand the club could have bought some new players, but there's no guarantee that a big money buy will bring success on the pitch.

I am sure Ipswich will bounce back. The potential is there. They have a great stadium, a hard core of support and the nucleus of a good team. Youngsters like Mark Brennan, Ian Cranson, Jason Dozell and Frank Yallop have a great future in the game. I'm sure it won't be long before the club is back challenging for honours at the top of the League once again.

10

Alive and Kicking in Monterrey

I had mixed emotions as I packed my bags for Mexico. The excitement and anticipation of the two months ahead was marred by the news, less than twenty-four hours earlier, that Ipswich had been relegated. I had arranged to travel to the airport with Bobby Robson, the England manager, who lived just round the corner from us.

Bobby had been the Ipswich manager for thirteen years and was as shocked and disappointed as I was. It was a sad time for both of us, and as we drove to meet the rest of the team at our hotel near Heathrow we inevitably talked as much about Ipswich Town as we did about the World Cup. He warned me that there would be increasing speculation about my future and we both wondered where I would be playing next season.

As soon as we joined up with the rest of the squad the talk was about the World Cup and nothing else. I was confident that England would do well in Mexico. We were the only European team to qualify with an unbeaten record, and in those eight games we scored twenty-one goals and conceded two. We hadn't lost in any game for a year – a run which included a 1–0 victory over the USSR in Tbilisi and a 2–1 victory over Scotland at Wembley where I had scored one of the goals.

Bobby Robson is renowned for his 'Colemanballs' style expressions. 'You can see the smell of the place,' he said when we arrived in America and 'feel the ultra ray violets' was another. He gave the lads a few laughs at his own expense, not always intentionally. When we landed at Colorado he was urging us to hurry up and collect our bags so we could move on to the hotel. 'Come on lads. Look sharp,' he said, and started handing out bags to players who were slow to collect them. He picked up another one, looked at the label and started bellowing: 'Peter Reid! Come on Peter. Collect your bag. Where's Peter?' The lads were trying to hide their smirks and then someone piped up: 'Actually he's still in England, boss. Everton are in the Cup Final and he's joining us next week!'

A few days later the boss had us rolling about again when he came down to breakfast and poured salt over his grapefruit thinking it was sugar. On another day he got lost playing golf. He said he had played the course when he visited Colorado before and reckoned he was in the mood for a good round. We were following and suddenly noticed that he had disappeared from sight. Eventually he was spotted miles away having taken a wrong turn at one of the greens. He couldn't understand it when he was disqualified.

The planning for Mexico had been impeccable. For our eight weeks away we brought everything including our own electric kettle, 1,000 sachets of shampoo, 600 bars of soap, air-fresheners, cough medicine, stomach medicine and skin medicine, nearly 4,000 tea-bags, 500 bars of chocolate, 108 bottles of HP Sauce, our own mustard, 144 tins of baked beans and our own games including Monopoly, Trivial Pursuit and Scrabble.

The kit list was incredible. In Mexico we had fifteen sets of white shirts, eight sets of our change blue shorts and six sets of our second change red shirts. We brought sixty goalkeepers' jerseys and more then four hundred pairs of England socks. Ominously the inventory also listed a wooden spoon!

The back up staff were superb. Our physio Fred Street and his assistant Norman Medhurst were inseparable. Fred is one of the most cheerful men I have ever met. Nothing was ever too much trouble for them.

Bobby Robson was quoted as saying we could win the World Cup and, although we didn't kid ourselves that it would be easy, you could sense that the players felt we were in with a chance.

Our preparation was well planned and we flew to our training camp in the United States with four weeks to get everything right for our opening game against Portugal. The English League season had finished just a few days before we left and most of us were tired. Some players, like West Ham's Alvin Martin, had played a game virtually every other day for the last three weeks. The Everton players weren't able to join us for another week. They still had to play in the FA Cup Final, which they lost to Liverpool. It had been a particularly gruelling season for them as they had finished runners-up to Liverpool in the League as well.

We were based at the US Air Force Academy in Colorado Springs. It was an ideal choice, situated in some magnificent mountain scenery and with excellent facilities. Altitude had been the major problem for us during our trip to Mexico City the previous summer and training at the Academy, which was 8,000 feet above sea level, helped us adapt to the conditions we could expect at a similar height during the later stages of the World Cup. It was also very hot up there which helped us when we came down to Monterrey and played in the opening phase.

The manager and Don Howe had worked out some tough training sessions for us. One of the main problems at altitude is that you become breathless very quickly and we were constantly monitored to see how we were adapting.

Another problem is that the speed and flight of the ball is different in the thin atmosphere. It travels much faster, as I found to my cost when I went in goal for a training match. Mark Hateley hit a shot from about fifteen yards which nearly broke my hand. It takes time for players to get their timing right and during the first few sessions we were hopeless. Every time a cross came in we would all jump and miss it. Defenders have to get into position early to meet high balls and even when it lands in front of you the bounce and pace off the pitch is different to the conditions we are used to at sea level.

It's important for players in international teams to get used to playing with each other and we had a couple of friendly games against the Academy, whom we beat 11–0, and South Korea – who had also qualified for Mexico – whom we beat 4–1. We flew to Los Angeles for another warm-up game against Mexico, Mark Hateley scoring twice and Peter Beardsley once as we won 3–0. Warm up were the right words. The temperature was in the upper eighties and the stadium was like an oven.

One of the highlights of our time in Colorado was when our wives joined us for a week. It gave the players a boost at just the right time. We were to be away from home for almost two months and there were obviously times when we felt homesick. I was sad that I missed my younger son Edward take his first steps. When I left England he was still crawling and when I got back home after the World Cup he was running about all over the place.

Eight weeks of all male company could become monastic, and having Rita with me for those days was like a second honeymoon. The hotel was fantastic and as these were some of the most important weeks of my career I was glad she was able to share a part of it. We were obviously sad when the wives went home. The World Cup was still two weeks away and I knew it could be another six weeks before I saw Rita and the boys. The Football Association had been absolutely fantastic in organizing the wives' trip and it was a tremendous gesture that all the players appreciated (apart from Gary Bailey and Steve Hodge who had no female partners and possibly another six weeks enforced celibacy to contend with).

There was no time to dwell on the departure of our wives. We left for a friendly against Canada in Vancouver which we won 1–0, and then went on to Mexico.

We had been drawn in Group F along with Poland, Portugal and Morocco, who were one of two African teams to qualify. Our games were to be played at Monterrey, an industrial city about 500 miles north of Mexico City and one of the hottest places in the country where temperatures would be up around 100°F for the start of our games.

Our opening game was against Portugal, who had looked a useful side during the 1984 European Championships when they reached the semi-finals before losing to France. They had also become the first team to beat West Germany in a World Cup qualifying game, winning 1–0 in Stuttgart. But recently there had been stories that their players were threatening to strike unless they were paid more money for their World Cup appearances.

Our team contained few surprises. Peter Shilton was in goal;

the defence had Everton's Gary Stevens and Kenny Sansom at full-back, with Terry Fenwick and me in the centre; Glenn Hoddle, Ray Wilkins and Bryan Robson were in midfield; Chris Waddle would play wide, with Mark Hateley and Gary Lineker up front. Gary played with his wrist protected after he sprained it badly in the friendly against Canada.

I felt more nervous before the Portugal game than I had felt for a long time. After so much work the big moment had finally arrived and we all knew that millions of people would be watching on television all over the world. As usual Gary Bailey brought his ghetto blaster on the coach. He's a nice enough man but his taste in music is different to mine. Gary likes George Benson and Whitney Houston, not the type of artists to appear in my heavy metal collection. I had planned it well and brought my own earphones to listen to some soothing AC/DC.

Even though our coach was air-conditioned I found myself sweating throughout the journey. The heat at the ground was unbearable, well over 100°F and the hottest day for weeks. We went out on to the pitch about forty minutes before the kick-off to get used to the flight of the ball and the atmosphere in the stadium and, just as importantly, to help ease the tension that had been building up. I was wearing my match shirt and when we went back to the dressing room it was soaked with sweat from just jogging around and casually knocking a few balls around.

We had trained at the Technological Stadium a few days earlier and had been disappointed at the state of the pitch which was very bumpy. The grass was long but it wasn't very thick and it was a difficult decision whether to wear studs and risk blisters or to wear moulded soles and risk losing your feet. I went for studs. To get to the pitch from the changing rooms you had to walk through a maze of hedges, a bit like going on court at Wimbledon.

Each player has his own routine before a game. I always put my left sock on before my right and put my shirt on last. Ray Wilkins likes to be the last person to put his shorts on. Bryan Robson always likes a shower before a game and Viv Anderson has a bath.

About fifteen minutes before we're due to go on to the pitch,

I like to sit in a corner with my head-phones and listen to some tapes which were made especially for me by an Ipswich doctor, Doc Lewis, who is also a hypnotherapist. There's just his voice on the tape and it helps me get in the right frame of mind for the game. It's all about positive thinking and a question of mind over matter.

The tapes help me control my mind by saying that although it's hot I'm not going to let it affect me. I drift into a trance for a while and when I come out of it I'm charged up and ready to go. The tapes seem to work and despite the temperatures I wasn't affected at all by the heat.

Doc's taped message had told me that the sun would be hot but it would act as a stimulant. Despite the heat I would be cool inside and ooze authority. I had been introduced to hypnotherapy by Bobby Ferguson who had commissioned Doc Lewis to talk to the Ipswich team the previous season. It is a system that is common among top sportsmen, but I was the only England player to use the technique.

The preparations had been so thorough and the spirit was so good as we went out for the game that none of us expected it to be such a disastrous result.

Portugal played with one man up front and packed five in midfield which made it hard for us to play. Chris Waddle was wide but found he had two or three men to beat whenever he got the ball. We were also looking to use Gary Lineker's pace and play balls over the top of their defence for him to run on to, but they had so many players defending there was no space to drop the ball in to.

With all routes forward blocked we were forced to play the ball square. Any openings we created were immediately closed down and we would have to play the ball out again and square once more. It was frustrating to watch and equally frustrating to play in.

With a massed midfield the Portuguese were also able to break quickly. Some players could push forward with others holding back to cover. It was a tactic which also stretched our defence pulling myself and Terry Fenwick apart. Terry was marking Gomes, the lone Portugal forward who was standing between him and Gary Stevens, our right-back. I was picking up runners from midfield and they were pulling me to the left leaving a gap in our centre.

It was a tactic we soon became accustomed to during the World Cup and when we played a four-man midfield in the later stages it was easier to combat.

At half-time although we hadn't found a way through the Portuguese defence they hadn't mounted a serious attack either. To help us cool down we wrapped cold towels round our body and drank about two pints of fluid each. Bobby Robson said he was pleased with the way things were going and if we were patient he was sure the goals would come.

We started the second half well and had our best spell of the game with Gary Lineker and Bryan Robson coming close to scoring. Then, against the run of play, Portugal scored. Diamantino broke on the right and beat Kenny Sansom. I hesitated instead of closing him down immediately and gave him the chance to put in a low cross which was turned past Peter Shilton by Carlos Manuel who was free on the far post. It was a bad goal to give away and the worst we had defended for a long time.

Peter Beardsley and Steve Hodge came on for Chris Waddle and Bryan Robson but we couldn't find a way to goal. I was booked for a lunging tackle on Futre, the Portuguese substitute. Frustration had got the better of me and it was a foolish thing to do. Bobby Robson was furious and I had put myself on a knife-edge for the rest of the tournament. 'It's not what I expect from an experienced international,' he said later.

We hadn't expected to lose to Portugal and the mood in the changing room was solemn. Everyone was quiet, some of the lads were close to tears and others sat with their heads in their hands. To make matters worse the showers were cold.

Bobby Robson and Don Howe tried to lift us saying: 'Come on, we've got two games to go. If we win those we can still win the group.'

The following day we had a long team meeting to clear the air before our next game against Morocco.

The result against Portugal did little to improve the condition of the team Doctor, Vernon Edwards, who had suffered a heart attack a few days earlier. Doc, a popular figure with the lads, had been with us in Spain and worked hard in preparing us for Mexico. His sudden illness upset us all and was the kind of thing we could have done without before such an important game.

Our next opponents, Morocco, had qualified for the Finals after beating Libya 3–1 on aggregate. They had surprised a few people already by drawing their opening game against Poland 0–0, where their skilful midfield players Timoumi and Bouderbala had caught the eye.

Bobby Robson kept the same side and we knew we had to play better than we had against Portugal. For some strange reason we didn't.

We were confident enough before the game and the plan was to take the game to the Moroccans and look for an early goal. But before we could get going we had lost both Bryan Robson, who aggravated his old shoulder injury, and Ray Wilkins who was sent off. I though Ray was unlucky. He had been booked earlier for obstruction and when he was given off-side in a good position in the Moroccan penalty-area he threw the ball away in frustration. When you consider some of the tackles by the Uruguayans that went unpunished throughout the tournament, Ray's dismissal was disgraceful but unfortunately typical of the inconsistency of the refereeing in Mexico.

Peter Shilton took over as our third captain of the game and at half-time he had a go at the rest of us who were still a bit dazed at having lost Bryan and Ray. Both he and the boss were telling us to forget about what had happened and concentrate on the forty-five minutes ahead of us.

Glenn Hoddle moved to the centre of midfield, where I think he should play all the time. He's the playmaker in our side and our equivalent of France's Michel Platini. Glenn has so much skill that no matter how tightly marked he is he always seems to be able to receive the ball and turn into space. He's also got the ability to hit balls into the areas that put defenders under pressure and can open routes to goal with his precise passing. He seemed to revel in his new responsibility and our ten men all played well in the second half.

The Moroccans were happy to defend and play the game in their own half despite having the extra man. It led to stalemate. With ten men we couldn't afford to push too many players forward in case we were caught on the break. Steve Hodge was already on for Bryan Robson and Tottenham's Gary Stevens came on for Mark Hateley to give us another man in midfield, confuse the commentators and provoke the chant from the England fans 'There's only two Gary Stevens'.

The game petered out into a o–o draw. The important thing was that we hadn't lost, but we had been hoping for four points from our first two games and instead had only one. At the end of the game we were supposed to go to the centre-circle, wave to the crowd and shake hands and swap shirts, but I was so disappointed I just wanted to get off as quickly as possible.

The Moroccan centre-half followed me and was shouting 'Boo-cha, Boo-cha Boo-cha!' I didn't feel like talking to anyone, but he followed me into our changing rooms. He was a big man and I wondered what he wanted, but when I looked round he was smiling all over his face and very politely said: 'Plees, Boo-cha, change shirt plees.'

We swapped shirts and as he ran out with a huge grin all over his face he passed the rest of the England team as they trudged back in looking tired, dejected and close to tears. Nobody said anything. Ray Wilkins looked heart-broken and Pop Robson, with his arm in a sling, sat quietly in a corner – it was a picture which summed up our plight. Our worst fears were becoming a reality and the prospect loomed that we might go out of the competititon after the first phase.

Bobby Robson probably felt as low as we did and knew that he would be savaged on television and in the newspapers, but he deserves credit for the way he lifted our spirits immediately. He went round saying 'Well done. We've got a draw and we're still in the competition. If we beat Poland then we're through to the next round.' It was easier said than done, but it was what we needed – some positive thinking before our negative thoughts took control.

We had five days to get the Morocco disaster out of our system. It's times like that when team spirit is important. You need to be able to lift each other when things are going wrong. Luckily we had a fantastic squad with a great bunch of lads. I don't think there were any arguments throughout the two months we were away.

As usual I was rooming with Viv Anderson, the Arsenal full-back, and it was his turn to cheer me up. He'd been very low before the first game when Everton's Gary Stevens was picked ahead of him. I thought Viv had played well in the run up to the competition, especially against Russia and Mexico, and he was unlucky to be left out. But he's so bubbly, humorous and talkative, that he soon bounces back. He fancies himself as a centre-forward and in training he always plays up front if he can. Whenever he scores you never hear the last of it! He'd keep me awake chatting until two o'clock some nights and then when I'd say something he would say: 'Oh come on, Butch. It's late. Let's go to sleep.'

Viv and I had clubbed together for a music centre before we went to Mexico. He's a Rolling Stones fanatic, which is fine, but he also likes bands like Go West, Talking Heads and George Benson. I made him wear head-phones when he played their tapes and I had to wear them when I played my heavy metal cassettes. I find it very relaxing to listen to a band like AC/DC with the volume right up, but Viv for some reason never appreciated it.

It's important to get on well with your room-mate if you are away for such a long time.

Bryan Robson and Ray Wilkins always share a room, and Gary Lineker was with Peter Shilton. The other goalies, Chris Woods and Gary Bailey, stuck together and Kenny Sansom and Glen Hoddle's room became known as the 'Bookies' as they were always taking bets on anything from televised football games to the squad pool competition, which was won by Gary Lineker who beat Terry Fenwick in the final.

Peter Beardsley had organized the competition. He became known as 'ceefax' because he seemed to know everything that was going on. He was a popular character who would do anything for anybody.

To show his confidence, Bobby Robson took us up into the mountains for altitude training to prepare for the second-round games even though we still had to beat Poland to qualify. We trained at an old monastery where the air was beautiful. It was a lovely setting and after a barbecue lunch we had an impromptu game of cricket. I'm quite an ordinary player, but both John Barnes and Glenn Hoddle were more than useful bowlers.

Since the Morocco game we had held a couple of meetings

where everyone said what they thought had gone wrong and what we should do to put it right. The football in our group overall had been dull. The locals called it 'the group of sleep' and Zbigniew Boniek, the Polish captain, had advised people to stay at home and watch television rather than go to the games. In the first four games there had been just two goals and very little for the football fanatics of Monterrey to cheer about. We hadn't scored in two games and we knew we had to beat Poland to go through to the last sixteen.

Ray Wilkins was suspended for two games and there had been a lot of guesses among the squad about the team the boss would pick. He announced it on the morning of the game, just five hours before kick-off. Although we were expecting changes it still came as a bit of a shock. He wanted us to play a 4-4-2 system, which some of the lads had wanted from the start, to combat the massed midfields we had encountered. Peter Reid was in for Ray and Steve Hodge came in for Bryan Robson, whose shoulder was still suspect. Trevor Steven replaced Chris Waddle and up front Peter Beardsley was chosen in place of Mark Hateley.

It's hard to look someone in the face when they've just been dropped. You know they are disappointed but you don't know what to say. To their credit both Chris and Mark took it well, staying chirpy and encouraging the lads who were playing.

That morning just before our team meeting the English papers had arrived with reports of our game against Morocco. We'd expected criticism but some of the attacks were vicious. A lot of the lads were angry, particularly at Emlyn Hughes who couldn't find a good thing to say about any of us. We thought: 'Right, we'll shut them up. We'll make them eat their words.' Apart from announcing the side, the manager did not need to gee us up – the comments from the so-called football experts were enough for that.

On the journey to the ground Gary Bailey's ghetto blaster was blaring out some Simple Minds and when the track 'Alive and Kicking' came on there was a big cheer from the lads as if to say: 'That's our song. We'll win today despite being written off in the press.'

There had been a lot of talk about the last time England had played Poland, back in October 1973. England needed to win to qualify for the World Cup Finals but could only draw 1–1. Most of the present England squad were too young to remember the game, although Peter Shilton could never forget it as he was in goal that day.

It was another hot day with the temperatures in the nineties. The game was at the University Stadium which had a better pitch than the Technological. The English supporters gave us a rousing reception when we went out on the pitch before the game and they seemed optimistic. All of us could sense the atmosphere building up. We went back into the cool of the dressing room for a quiet ten minutes before the kick-off. Peter Shilton was skipper for the day and kept reminding us that he had never lost as England captain. There was none of the usual banter, but everyone knew how important this game was. I have never seen an England team go out for a game as determined to win as we were that day.

We started slowly and Poland created a couple of chances. The most worrying was when Boniek broke free, Shilts parried his shot and the ball broke loose in front of our open goal. I was just able to stretch out and touch the ball back to Shilts and prevent Smolarek from getting the vital contact.

That scare seemed to jolt us and then we put together one of the best moves of the game to take the lead. The build-up involved Kenny, Glenn, Gary Lineker and Peter Beardsley before Peter Reid put Trevor Steven in space on the right. He knocked it for Gary Stevens, who was on an overlap, and his first time cross behind the Polish sweeper was tucked home by Gary Lineker.

Six minutes later Gary Lineker scored again after a move involving Peter Beardsley and Steve Hodge. He completed his hat-trick after thirty-five minutes from a corner and the game was virtually over. You could feel the relief running through the team. We started believing in ourselves again and the confidence flowed back.

At last we were playing the football we knew we were capable of. Poland hadn't conceded a goal in their first two matches but we were looking dangerous with every attack. At half-time the boss and Don were rushing about trying to calm us down. We sat swathed in cold towels and swilling our special drinks, as they impressed on us the need to make sure that the Poles weren't given a chance to come back at us.

With the exception of a couple of shots from Boniek they didn't. Our 4–4–2 formation meant the midfield were not getting overwhelmed, and it made life better for us at the back where we could read the game more easily and consequently were much tighter. There wasn't such a big gap between the defence and the midfield and we were able to deny the Poles any space.

We knew Boniek was the danger man and that he liked to run with the ball. But we had closed down the space so quickly that he had nowhere to run. He had a couple of shots near the end, one hit the post and Peter Shilton saved the other, but he kept on trying. Towards the end he said to me: 'It is 3–0 to England. You let me score just one goal please!' I smiled at him and just said: 'No chance.'

Boniek's main asset is his speed, but he's also got a quick brain. He knows when to use his pace and it gets him into some good positions. Unlike some nippy players who do the hard work and then waste their chance he's got a calm head and is a good finisher. He's also quite a character and we met him at a reception before the tournament where he was saying the Polish team had banned alcohol but the players were desperate for a beer.

It was a great team display from England. Our pace up front had caused problems and when we were defending there was always a back up when going in for a tackle. The English fans had been marvellous. There were about 4,000 in the ground and after the second goal they started doing the 'conga' around the stadium. They were behind us from the start and it made us feel at home. After the Morocco game a number of them had jeered our coach as we left the stadium. Their support until then had been fantastic and we were disappointed that we hadn't given them more to cheer about. After the Poland game we could hear them singing long after the final whistle had blown.

The atmosphere in the dressing room was jubilant and a staggering contrast to the mood after our previous two games. Everyone was on a high and the lads who hadn't played were as happy as the rest of us. It felt as though a two ton weight had been lifted off our shoulders. On the coach journey back to Saltillo, we banned George Benson and instead had a Beatles sing-along. Even Don Howe joined in.

We finished second in our group. Morocco beat Portugal 3–1 to finish top while Poland came third. Portugal, who'd been so euphoric after beating us in the first game came bottom and went out of the competition. It couldn't have been better if we had planned it from the start. Morocco's reward for finishing top was a tough game against West Germany in Monterrey, Poland met Brazil; while we had the best draw of the lot, Paraguay at the Azteca Stadium in Mexico City.

We had a week to prepare for the game which gave us plenty of time to leave our comfortable hotel in Saltillo, where everyone had made us feel at home, and acclimatize ourselves in Mexico City. Most of the squad had been there the year before, but since then the city had been badly hit by an earthquake.

In the Mexican earthquake more than 6,000 people were killed, twice as many injured and about 50,000 were left homeless. It caused extensive damage to buildings throughout the city and, although the worst had been cleared up, whole buildings were missing along some of the main roads. It often seemed incongruous that with so many Mexicans living in poverty the country should stage the World Cup which cost millions of pounds to put on.

Our first hotel was a huge disappointment. It was on a busy main road and there was so much noise during the night that none of us could get a decent night's sleep. To make matters worse the beds were too small and neither Mark Hateley nor I had any chance of sleeping.

For our main meal we were served a small piece of fried fish, one boiled potato and six slices of carrot each, followed by a slim wedge of dried cake for dessert. It was nowhere near enough for a group of hungry footballers and once we'd finished most of us went off to a hamburger bar for a second meal. There was uproar. The new team doctor, John Crane, wanted to know why we were eating stodgy food when we should be on special diets, but he was sympathetic when we told him what we'd been offered at the hotel.

To avoid a mutiny arrangements were made for us to move to another hotel. Everyone was delighted until we heard it was close to the airport and we had more misgivings about sleepless nights, but it turned out to be an excellent choice and the aeroplanes never disturbed us.

The time between games can be tough for players. Training was in the morning and usually lasted about an hour and a half. The rest of the day was our own. Because of the high security surrounding the England squad we weren't able to just get up and go out for a walk. A few of the lads went sightseeing and visited the Aztec pyramids at Teotihuacan, but most of us spent our time in the hotel so it was important that we had comfortable rooms to rest in. If they aren't comfortable then you end up running around doing things you shouldn't. Some experts say rest is as important as training for footballers. It may appear to be a glamorous world but there seem to be endless hours of boredom killing time between games.

Most of us played at the Azteca Stadium during our tour the previous year. At that time the changing rooms were dark, dismal and flooded regularly. Work was going on throughout the stadium to prepare it for the World Cup and it looked as though it would never be ready. The pitch was surrounded by rubble and the stadium had been a disappointment to those of us who had heard how impressive it was supposed to be.

When we went back for the Paraguay game it had changed completely. The changing rooms were immaculate and the stadium was full of colour with flags and decorations everywhere. We trained there two days before the game and were surprised at how wet the pitch was. It was hard to keep your feet in places and one corner was particularly slippery where players kept falling over throughout the competition.

As soon as you arrive for a game at the Azteca Stadium the atmosphere hits you. Even in the changing room you can hear a cacophony of trumpets, horns and drums, all making a bigger din than Black Sabbath. And when the teams go on to the pitch the noise is quite deafening. The English fans were doing their best to compete and we saw hundreds of Union Jacks. I even spotted one banner from my home town of Lowestoft.

As expected the boss kept faith with the team that had beaten Poland with one change, Alvin Martin replacing Terry Fenwick who was suspended. Dave Sexton had watched Paraguay and we knew their style was more European than South

American. They played with two men up front and we worked on combating their system in training.

Paraguay had already beaten Iraq and drawn with Mexico and Belgium. Their midfield player Julio Cesar Romero was the South American Footballer of the Year and up front Roberto Cabanas had scored twice against the Belgians, so we knew it wasn't going to be easy. The manager, Cayetano Re, had been shown the red card during the Belgium game for constant encroachment and dissent, and at one time during the match the referee was surrounded by ten of their players involved in a fracas with a couple of Belgium players.

Once again we had a couple of scares early on, and I was involved in both. First Romero slipped a ball square to Mendoza on the half-way line and he showed an amazing burst of speed to break clear. He was through on goal but just delayed his shot long enough for me to slide in with a tackle. It was a crucial moment and I was pleased to have recovered in time.

Then I nearly gave a goal away with a disastrous pass back which was cut out by Mendoza. Peter Shilton did superbly and forced him wide without bringing him down. When Mendoza squared the ball, Canete's close-range shot was knocked straight at Shilts. We were lucky to get away with it. Apparently everyone had been shouting at me to knock it away, but I hadn't heard anything above the din of the horns and the crowd. To my left Kenny was marked and there was nothing on up front. I could see Shilts out of the corner of my eye and thought it was safe. I couldn't believe it when Mendoza came into the picture. .

Instead of being two down we went a goal up. Glenn Hoddle curled a ball across their goal. Gary Lineker lunged for it with a defender, missed it and ended up on the ground. Steve Hodge was lurking beyond the far post and did well to cut it back past the keeper and Gary just got up in time to turn it in.

We took control after that and the Paraguayans resorted to some rough stuff. One of their defenders elbowed Gary Lineker in the throat. Gary went down in obvious pain and they were claiming that he was pretending to be hurt. Gary was stretchered off and play restarted with a corner. Alvin Martin and I were at the far post. Alvin said: 'I'll go first,' and was off. The ball was flicked on and fell on my right foot. My first touch put the ball exactly where I wanted and I span and cracked a shot as hard as I could. As I fell I saw the keeper drop the ball and Peter Beardsley nipped in to score. It was an important goal and a tremendous feeling for me to have a hand in it.

Paraguay turned up the rough stuff. One of their defenders punched me in the throat at a corner, his fist landing directly on my Adams apple. I struggled to keep my cool as I had been booked against Portugal and another caution for a wild reaction would have meant an automatic ban. Instead I just pointed at the offender and snarled as if to say: You wait until the next corner, I'm going to have you. The referee intervened and calmed us down. I cannot stand kicks, punches and niggles off the ball and if the referee fails to do anything about them I am tempted to take the law into my own hands. I know its wrong but there's no justice in people getting away with constant digs. There were no more corners that game, but at least that player didn't foul anyone again.

I was delighted when we scored our third goal to finish off the Paraguayans. It was a lovely move with Glenn Hoddle playing a ball inside the full-back setting his Tottenham team-mate, Gary Stevens, through. Gary didn't even need to look up when he crossed the ball. He just knew Gary Lineker would be there to score.

At the end of the game I refused to swap shirts with any of the Paraguayan players. I was so angry at the way they had played that I didn't want anything to do with them. Bobby Robson and Don Howe tried to change my mind. They said: 'Come on, the game's over. You've got to be a sportsman and swap shirts.' I thought: But I am a sportsman, that's the whole point. My England shirt means more to me than a Paraguayan. So I kept mine.

It had been another good team performance. We'd overcome the depression and dejection following our first two games and now we were through to the last eight in the world.

11

'The Hand of God'

All that now stood between England and a place in the World Cup semi-finals was Argentina. Inevitably before the game there was endless talk about the Falklands. As soon as we had beaten Paraguay, journalists were asking Bobby Robson questions along those lines. He warned the players not to get drawn. 'Just say it's history and has nothing to do with football.'

We trained once more at the Azteca and tried to practise there again on the day before the game, but that episode turned into a morning of farce rather than football. When we arrived at the stadium the officials wouldn't let us in. They said they weren't expecting us and in any case, because it had rained the night before, FIFA said neither us or Argentina could train on the pitch. Nobody from FIFA had told us this but the Azteca officials were adamant. There was a right old hoo-ha.

After arguing for about an hour, someone suggested we go to the Atlantic stadium and train there. It was half an hour away and we'd used it a couple of times before. Wherever the England coach went we had a police escort with cars, outriders, sirens and flashing lights, the lot. So the whole convoy turned round to head off through the city once more.

When we arrived at the stadium that too was locked and there was nobody to let us in. It was the kind of mix-up you may expect with a Sunday morning pub side, but not for a team just twenty-four hours away from a World Cup quarter-final. The players had been on the coach for two hours and were pulling their hair out in frustration. It was approaching the hottest part of the day, we'd been driving around Mexico City all morning and we just wanted to forget about training and go back to our hotel and relax, watching the game between France and Brazil on television.

Then a policeman came along to pick the lock and let us in. We had to climb over fences and down the terraces to get on to the pitch and, as we couldn't get into the changing rooms, we had to strip off in the goal-mouth. We trained for about half an hour and, as the dressing rooms were still locked, we had to clamber back up the terracing and on to the coach in our sweaty kit for the drive back to the hotel. Looking back I can see the funny side, but at the time it was frustrating and the last thing we needed before such a big game.

Argentina had finished top of their first round group, beating South Korea and Bulgaria and drawing with Italy. In the second round they beat Uruguay 1–0. Maradona in particular had looked dangerous, running directly at defenders and beating three or four men before laying off some superb passes for his colleagues.

If we won, the FA had promised to fly out our wives for the semi-finals and that gave us an added incentive, as if we needed one. It's a funny feeling when you are in the quarter-finals. You are so close to success and I couldn't help thinking that if we beat Argentina we would only have to win two more games to be assured of footballing immortality.

We were in a different changing room for the Argentina game. Most of would have preferred to keep the one we had used against Paraguay. It had been lucky for us once and footballers are generally a superstitious bunch. The noise inside the stadium was even more deafening than before, with more than 114,000 creating an electric atmosphere. As we went on to the pitch I was amazed at the number of Argentina flags and banners which seemed to be everywhere, easily out-numbering the pockets of England fans who were doing their best to make themselves heard.

The manager had made one change to the team, with Terry Fenwick coming back from his one-match suspension to replace Alvin Martin. There had been doubts about Peter Reid, who had an ankle injury, and Gary Lineker, who had a groin strain, but both recovered and were passed fit. We knew that Gary, with five goals already and the tournament's leading scorer, would worry the Argentina defence.

Twenty years earlier England had met Argentina in the quarter-finals and had won 1–0 before going on to win the World Cup. There were a few of us praying that history would repeat itself.

The first time we saw the Argentina team was when we met in the tunnel before the game. I remember thinking they looked confident and were raring to go, whereas the other sides we had met, such as Poland and Paraguay, didn't have that sense of urgency and had tended to look apprehensive. And once the game started Argentina were strong and aggressive while we were the opposite, giving the ball away and often negative in our play.

Neither side created a clear chance and at half-time the score was still 0–0. As we wrapped ourselves in the customary cold towels, Bobby Robson said we had to step up another ten per cent and show more determination. 'The first goal could settle this game,' he said. And although we started the next half well it was Argentina who scored.

It is probably the most talked-about goal of the tournament. Having seen the replays on television there is no doubt that Maradona punched the ball in, but at the time I have to admit that I didn't see him handle it. I was level with Steve Hodge and saw the midfielder play the ball over his head and back to Peter Shilton. I remember thinking: That's Shilts', but the next thing I saw was the ball bouncing into the empty net. I naturally thought the Argentinian star had headed it, and was standing there in amazement when Peter Shilton and Glenn Hoddle flashed past me running towards the referee screaming 'Hand-ball, hand-ball!' The referee just waved them away and said it was a goal.

I don't think you can blame the referee for not seeing it. He had the same view as I had. As I have said before, I didn't see Maradona's hand connect with the ball as it was shielded from my view by his head. But if the referee didn't see the vital contact then the linesman must have done. The ball was in the air for quite a long time and he had an unimpeded view, yet he didn't raise his flag. If there was a doubt about the goal, the referee should have consulted the linesman but he didn't seem to bother.

Later in the game during a lull in play I asked Maradona if he had handled the ball. He just smiled and pointed to his head. Later, of course, he was quoted as saying that the goal was scored a little 'by the hand of God and a little by the head of Maradona'.

Everyone says how brilliant Maradona's second goal was, but from our point of view it was dreadful. He ran from the half-way line beating four of us before side-stepping Peter Shilton and scoring. He should really have been stopped long before he reached our penalty-area. I am as guilty as anyone and should have tackled or even up-ended him, but I didn't shape up to make a move and he went past me too easily. Then he went past Terry Fenwick, who had already been booked and couldn't bring him down for fear of being sent off. As Maradona went past Peter Shilton, I tried to get in a tackle but couldn't see the ball and, unfortunately for us, he got his foot to it and scored.

A lot of teams wouldn't have let him run that far and maybe we paid the penalty for not being cynical. An Italian, for example, would probably have brought him down at the half-way line before he could reach the danger area.

There is no doubt that Maradona has exceptional skill. He is short and stocky and has electrifying pace over the first five or six yards. Sometimes his speed gets him into trouble, but most of the time it helps him out of it. He's got tiny feet which also make him nimble and when a big chap commits himself to tackle he can push the ball past with a couple of extra touches and burst free. He is hard to mark because he is so quick. He can improvise to get out of any hole, and no matter how many players surround him he'll come away with the ball.

Maradona rarely does the expected and his vision and passing is tremendous, weighting balls perfectly and making it easy for a colleague all the time. But what I don't like about him is the inevitable dive whenever he is tackled. There were times when we would win the ball fairly, but Maradona would go tumbling over and win a free-kick. That kind of thing happened regularly in Mexico and it left a bad taste in my

mouth. You could see players making a meal out of fair challenges and then start rolling about when you knew that they
weren't hurt. They would wait for the defender to be booked
and then be up and run around as right as rain.

Such play acting doesn't happen very often in British football
and I don't think the fans here would stand for it. They soon
start jeering if a player feigns the slightest injury.

Perhaps we conceded the second goal because our minds
were still on the first, but even though we were 2–0 down we
still felt we were in with a chance and at last we started to
play. We were shouting and encouraging each other and we
played our best football of the match. Chris Waddle and John
Barnes came on and both stayed wide, causing problems for
the Argentina defence. John pulled one superb cross back from
near the corner flag for Gary Lineker to score.

Pumpido, the Argentina goalkeeper, made a good save
pushing a Glenn Hoddle free-kick against the post, and I had
a header from a corner which he also saved. One of their
defenders had been putting his elbow in my face to stop me
making a run and, having got into a tangle with him and
Terry Fenwick's marker, the ball came straight to me on the
far post. I had no time to react positively, the header lacked
any power and Pumpido saved easily.

Argentina had broken away and hit our post, but we continued to press and once again John Barnes whipped in another
superb cross. It looked to be going in until an Argentinian
defender dived headlong towards his own goal and somehow
bounced the ball off his back to safety. That touch was enough
to stop Gary Lineker scoring to send the game into extra-time
and it meant that Argentina and not us were through to the
semi-finals.

The World Cup had been my life for every moment of every
day for the last eight weeks. Suddenly it was over and I felt
empty and sad. Some of the players exchanged shirts – Steve
Hodge swapped with Maradona – but I just wanted to get
back to the privacy of our changing room. Some people have
criticized me for not waving to the fans after the game as the
FIFA regulations say players should do. It's not that I don't
appreciate the fans and the support they gave us. I do and they
were tremendous but I was close to tears, bitterly disappointed

and felt as though we had let everyone down. To go and wave as if everything was fine would seem as though I didn't care about the result.

I made for the changing room, but a Mexican official blocked my path. I was in no mood to be messed about and was set to flatten him when someone explained that he was pointing to the dope-testing room. Three players are drawn from each team and my number had come up.

I sat in a green room all alone for about five minutes before Kenny Sansom and Everton's Gary Stevens came in. It was a small room with benches on either side and a fridge stocked with drinks. We sat there, heads in hands, staring at the wall opposite. Then the door burst open and the Argentina players who had been drawn came in – Maradona, Brown and one of the substitutes – singing, shouting and hugging each other. Then a FIFA official came in and hugged Maradona. I thought: Bloody hell, he scored the first goal by cheating and the officials come in to congratulate him.

We could hear the Argentina celebrations, but by contrast our changing room was quiet. When I arrived back the lads were sitting in silence with glum faces. Don Howe was walking around, dazed, saying: 'All that work and a bloke comes along and punches the ball in the net and that's it.'

I sat and thought: All that effort, all that time and all the money that's been spent, all for nothing. All I wanted was to get home and see my family.

Argentina went on to beat Belgium 2–0 in the semi-final, with Maradona scoring two brilliant goals. In the final he was more subdued, but still made the pass that set Burruchaga free to score the winner after West Germany had pulled the game back to 2–2.

I was impressed with Argentina throughout the tournament and had tipped them as likely winners early on. We heard a lot about Maradona, but they had a strong side with quality players in every position.

Argentina are a hard team to play against. They pack their midfield and defence and try to suck in their opponents and catch them on the break. They switch from defence to attack so quickly, with two or three precision passes and they are up the other end with a chance on goal.

Jorge Valdano, who plays in Spain for Real Madrid, and scored Argentina's second goal in the final, is a typical strong centre-forward. Often he had to plod away on his own up front, but it's hard to get the ball off him. He'll tackle and knock you about like an English or Scottish centre-forward, and players like Burruchaga, Maradona and Enrique are able to feed off him.

Pumpido, the goalkeeper, made some important saves and their defence was solid. The only time they looked vulnerable was when John Barnes came on and went wide putting in crosses from near the corner flag. In the final both German goals came from corners in the same spot.

There was a lot of talk about how hard it is for a European team to win the World Cup in South America. The finals have been held there six times and on each occasion a South American team has won. I don't think it will be long before a European team breaks that run. They came close this time with three teams reaching the semi-finals. Before the competition I had felt confident about England's chances and, if we failed, I fancied France to go all the way.

Preparations are important and all the teams adopted a more scientific approach this time. Our build up was ideal and the altitude training in Colorado helped us adapt to conditions in Mexico City without any problem.

The game is different in South America. To begin with the pitches have long grass whereas in Europe we tend to keep it short. It means that in South America the ball will not run so far. The style of play is also different. In Europe the game is played at a faster pace, in South America we found they adopted a slow, patient build up before a sudden burst of speed into attack.

It's easier for England to play European teams as we have probably come up against their players once or twice before, either for our clubs or in an international. Against South American teams we generally encounter their players for the first time. There may be a few who play in Europe, but more often the only time you've seen them before is on television.

A lot of the teams played with just one man up front and packed their midfield. It was something we came across in

Spain in 1982 and it took us a while to adapt. We normally play with a back four, while continental defences will have a sweeper and one defender who marks man-to-man allowing the spare defenders to push forward and flood the midfield when necessary.

I have always preferred playing against a big centre-forward because I know that I have someone to mark and keep out of the game. But adjusting to the changing tactics in the World Cup made me a better player, as you have to think and talk more about what is going on. You can't afford to lose concentration for one minute as the slightest lapse could cost a goal.

We also had to adjust our tactics going forward. Against eight or nine-man defences we found that playing the ball into the feet of our forwards resulted in little more than them being kicked and battered by defenders. Then, when we became frustrated, we started knocking high balls in which were obviously eaten up by world class defenders.

The changes we made against Poland enabled us to play the ball wide and push down the flanks. It's easier to do that with four in midfield and Trevor Steven, Steve Hodge and both full-backs were able to make some good runs and play in crosses which lead to goals.

We also learnt to be patient in our build up and keep possession until we were around the opposition penalty-area and then push the right pass in. Glenn Hoddle was a good example. He had the confidence to be patient and then release the ball at just the right moment and did just that to set up our third goal against Paraguay. I think the whole squad came back better players.

Once again Scotland were on a hiding to nothing. In 1982 their first-round group included Brazil and the USSR, who were two of the strongest teams in the competition. In Mexico it was even tougher as they were drawn with Uruguay, who were the South American champions, West Germany and Denmark. It soon became known as 'the group of death'.

There's always a great deal of interest in Scotland's progress among the England players. We were in Colorado when their squad was announced and I phoned my wife Rita to find out who was in and who'd been left out. Viv Anderson, my room-mate, was so keen to find out whether Charlie Nicholas, his Arsenal team-mate, was included that we didn't have time for the normal 'Hello darling, I miss you' stuff. Before Rita could say 'Hello' we were shouting 'What's the Scotland squad?'

There were several surprises, with Kenny Dalglish missing through injury and David Speedie of Chelsea and Liverpool's Alan Hansen both left out, but Viv was delighted when he heard that Charlie had made it.

I thought Charlie was one of the best players in the first game against Denmark until he was 'done' by a dreadful tackle from behind by Berggren. The referee booked the Dane but should really have sent him off. I was watching on television with Viv and we both winced at the tackle. It looked as though Charlie had been seriously hurt but he came back in time for the third game against Uruguay when he was substitute.

We all thought Scotland were unlucky to lose to Denmark, Preben Elkjaer scoring the game's only goal. Against West Germany I thought Scotland were on their way when Gordon Strachan put them one up. But West Germany never accept that they are beaten and went on to win 2–1, even though it looked as though David Narey had his shirt pulled by Rudi Voller to stop him tackling Allofs as he scored the winner.

Scotland needed to win their final game against Uruguay to go through to the second round, but the game was a disappointment. I thought Uruguay's tactics were shameful. They had a player sent off after fifty seconds for scything down Gordon Strachan, but continued their brutal form of tackling for the next eighty-nine minutes. The Scotland manager, Alex Ferguson, called them a 'disgrace to football' and it's hard to disagree. Their tactics, described perfectly in one report as 'organized brutality', added nothing to the competition.

A 0–0 draw meant that Uruguay and not Scotland went through. Not many people were sorry to see them lose to Argentina. They had already lost 6–1 to Denmark, and it seems wrong that a team beaten so convincingly should go through to the second round. They have some skilful players but they rarely showed their ability.

Northern Ireland were unable to repeat their performance of 1982 and failed to qualify for the second round, but I was delighted that Colin Clarke had a good World Cup and scored against Spain. Colin grew up in my home town of Lowestoft and trained for a while at Ipswich. His parents were interviewed on Anglia Television along with my parents to celebrate the first time that two Lowestoft lads had appeared in the World Cup finals.

Colin didn't make it at Ipswich, and after several years with Peterborough, Tranmere and Bournemouth he has seized his chance of First Division football with Southampton.

It was also Pat Jennings' last World Cup after winning a record 119 caps. He retired from the game on his forty-first birthday in Northern Ireland's final game against Brazil. It wasn't a thoroughly happy birthday as they lost 3–0, but there was one fantastic save, one-handed from Junior, followed by a brave block from Casagrande that showed he was still one of the best in the world.

The Mexican team was carried along on the human wave that the fans were so fond of. The support they had was fantastic. When they won, the entire population of Mexico City took to the streets to celebrate. Before the tournament everyone was expecting great things from Hugo Sanchez. His face popped up everywhere on advertising hoardings and television promoting soft drinks. He is a very good player and very dangerous in the penalty-area. But the pressure seemed to get to him and he didn't play to his full potential. He even missed a penalty against Paraguay with just minutes to play. As soon as the game was over another of his adverts came on the television, ironically with him taking a penalty. The Mexicans who were watching with us greeted him with derision and Hugo's image was slightly tarnished.

The Mexican public are fanatical about their football. Their love of the human wave caught us by surprise to begin with. A section of the crowd stand up and wave their arms about and shout 'Hola'. Then, as they sit down, the section next to them stands up and shouts and as they sit down the next section stands and so on. It gives the effect of a wave passing round the ground and is an impressive sight when in full swing around the Azteca. When I first heard it I thought there was trouble in the crowd, but it was something we soon got used to and it helped create a fantastic atmosphere.

I thought France were the pick of the European teams and

I scored twenty-one goals for Ipswich Town in 351 games. Here I am celebrating the last in my final home game for the club – the second goal in our 3–2 win over Oxford United...

...and that's how I did it. A right-foot volley as well!

The start of a new era as I sign for Rangers with my new boss Graeme
Souness (*left*), and the Chief Executive, David Holmes (*centre*).

The opening game at Easter Road was a turbulent affair. The gaffer got sent
off and I was shown the yellow card.

I love games where I'm in the thick of the action and in 'Old Firm' matches there's always total commitment from both teams.

Skol Cup winners 1986. The Rangers team after our 2–1 win over Celtic. Back row (*from left to right*): David MacFarlane, Derek Ferguson, Ted McMinn, Stuart Munro and Jimmy Nicholl. Front row: Ally Dawson, Robert Fleck, Chris Woods, Ian Durrant, Terry Butcher, Cammy Fraser and Davie Cooper.

An honorary 'Jock'…

…and a City whizz kid at the launch of my insurance business.

At home with my wife Rita and the boys Edward (*left*) and Christopher.

The goal that won the title – my header at Pittodrie on 2 May 1987.

Champions of Scotland.

The England v. Scotland game means as much to the players south of the border as it does to the Scots. Glenn Hoddle and I celebrate with the Rous Cup after scoring England's goals in our 2–1 win against Scotland at Wembley in 1986.

Lending support to Gary Lineker in Mexico. Gary was in at the deep end throughout our World Cup campaign in 1986 and emerged as the competition's leading scorer with six goals.

The end of England's World Cup dream. Maradona slips past Peter Shilton
and evades my desperate tackle to score Argentina's second goal in our
quarter-final game in Mexico City's Azteca Stadium. Minutes earlier he'd
punched the ball into the net for Argentina's first goal. Gary Lineker pulled
one back but we lost 2–1.

This picture sums up the way I felt after that second Maradona goal!

Being picked for the Rest of the World team against the Americas in July 1986 was a tremendous honour. I scored our first goal with a header and then spent much of the game marking Roberto Cabanas, the Paraguayan forward, who told me he wanted to play in England.

should have won the Cup. I hate to imagine what their changing room was like after losing to West Germany in the semi-final for the second time in four years.

France's strength was built on a marvellous defence and a superb midfield. Battiston and Bossis work well together at the back. Both are strong, brave and good in the air and neither likes to be beaten. They are good tacklers and when they've won the ball they use it intelligently.

In midfield they had so many gifted players able to run at pace with the ball. Tigana, Giresse and Platini can all beat people with ease, but Fernandez stood out for me as their key player. While Platini would stroll back after an attack broke down, Fernandez was willing to chase and tackle, win the ball and bring it forward again.

Rocheteau was missing in the semi-final, but although he looks flamboyant he tends to drift in and out of games. When he's on form he can be dynamic and hard to tie down. Against Italy he didn't seem to do much, but still set up two goals to help win the game.

West Germany never accept that they are beaten. They had a poor run before the World Cup and their manager Franz Beckenbauer, who was being criticized in the press, was in turn criticizing his players. There were stories of unrest in their camp and Uli Stein, the Hamburg goalkeeper, was sent home for saying that the team were playing like a bunch of 'cucumbers' whatever that meant.

Despite all that, West Germany reached the final. Their early form didn't suggest that they would do that well. A goal five minutes from time scraped a 1–1 draw with Uruguay. They snatched a 2–1 victory over Scotland and then lost 2–0 to Denmark. In the second round they met Morocco in a dour game, with Lothar Mattheus of Bayern Munich sneaking the winner from a free-kick two minutes from time.

In the quarter-finals against Mexico, West Germany seemed to be on their way out when Berthold was sent off in the sixty-fifth minute. Mexico controlled the game and only some fine saves from Schumacher kept Germany alive. Then, in extra-time Mexico lost their extra man advantage when Aguirre was sent off. The German strength and confidence showed through when the game went to penalties and they won 4–1. The

Mexicans looked scared and missed, the Germans looked confident and scored. They are such a strong side and keep going
even when things are against them that they score a lot of late
goals through sheer persistence. In the final West Germany
had looked out of the game at 2–0 down, but still pulled back
to 2–2 before Argentina scored the winner.

One of the surprise sides was Belgium, who finished third
behind Mexico and Paraguay in their first-round group but
went on to reach the semi-finals. Their 4–3 win over the USSR
was one of the most exciting games of the competition. Jan
Ceulemans, their captain, was the star of the side along with
Eric Gerets at the back. I met Eric when he played for Standard
Liege against Ipswich in a tournament in Amsterdam and he's
a smashing man. We went out to a few night clubs and he
was always ready for a few beers. He speaks quite good English
and always has a chat whenever we meet.

Their victory against the USSR was one of the upsets of the
tournament, as the Soviets were one of the favourites to win
the cup. They were a different team to the one we beat in
Tbilisi the previous March and, with five new faces and a new
manager, they out-classed Hungary 6–0 in the first round
scoring some marvellous goals. One of the joys about playing
the USSR is that they don't argue with the referee or roll about
pretending to be injured. If they are tackled they get up and
get on with the game.

Denmark went out in the second round when many people
were hoping that their flair would take them to the final.
Elkjaer and Laudrup had scored some lovely goals, but the
team fell to pieces against Spain and they lost 5–1.

Italy, the defending champions, never got going. We met
them in a hotel in Mexico City before their game against
France and they were slouching around looking anything but
potential world champions. I was surprised at the large number
of their team who smoked

Against France, the Italians seemed to accept that they
would lose, and apart from De Napoli and Di Gennaro, who
both seem to be exciting finds, it was a disappointing World
Cup for them.

Once again Brazil flattered to deceive. Like Italy their supporters hate to see their team lose. We've heard that when

Italy lose hundreds of supporters have been known to smash up their television sets in frustration. In Brazil the supporters are so fanatical that the whole country seems to stop when they have a World Cup match. After they lost to France on penalties newspapers reported that at least four people died of heart attacks and more than a hundred people were treated for severe shock in Rio de Janeiro.

Brazil seemed to be coming to the boil when they met France, but they were unfortunate to meet the on-form side for the second time in four years after losing to Italy in 1982. It was probably the best game of the World Cup, with end-to-end football and some great skills on display. I'm a great admirer of the Brazilian style, which they seem to improvise as they go along.

I played against two Brazilian teams for Ipswich. We met Vasco de Gama in America and Sao Paulo in Spain and their style was totally different to the European game. Players were free to float about in search of the ball, play quick one-twos anywhere on the pitch and always go forward looking for goals. It's all off the cuff, which makes it good to watch and hard to play against. Players are willing to take defenders on and shoot. If they don't score then at least they've had a go. Too many Europeans think: 'I can't beat the defender to shoot so I'll pass back or play the ball square.' But if you don't shoot you don't score.

In another twenty years I'm convinced that teams from Africa and the Middle East will have a good chance of winning the World Cup. In the late 1970s Ipswich often played friendlies in Dubai, Kuwait and Saudi Arabia and the game over there has come on leaps and bounds. Just before the World Cup Ipswich went to Iraq and played their second team twice. We won the first game 1–0 and drew the second 0–0 and came up against some skilful players.

Morocco and Algeria have some great ball players. In 1982 Algeria beat West Germany and in 1986 Morocco finished top of their group and, although European and South American teams will maintain their own standards, it won't be long before other countries catch up.

As a defender one of the things that made me angry in Mexico was the number of players who would roll about on the ground feigning injury after a tackle. Maradona wasn't the only culprit. We accept that players shouldn't kick lumps out of forwards and nobody condones the Uruguayan tactics, but referees should be able to distinguish between fair tackles and those designed to hurt a player with no intention of winning the ball.

Time wasting was another problem. You can often tell whether a South American side is winning without knowing the score purely by the time their players stay down after being tackled. If they get up immediately it's a fair bet that they are losing. If they stay down you can put your money on them being ahead. This blatant time wasting went on throughout the World Cup and few referees were prepared to do anything about it.

FIFA's attempt to stop it by rushing a stretcher on to carry off the injured player didn't save much time either. Players soon worked out you could waste even more time. A wall of team-mates would stand between the stretcher-bearers and the player on the floor to prevent him being carried off and waste a few more seconds. Inevitably the player would be fine and when he slowly rose to his feet even more time would be wasted while the stretcher-bearers ran off empty handed.

In our game against Argentina the time wasting that went on was disgraceful. Every time the ball went out of play we had to wait as the seconds ticked by before they restarted the game. In Mexico there were lengthy stoppages in most games, but few matches had any injury-time added on at the end. It's been suggested that the television companies put pressure on FIFA not to go over the allotted ninety minutes so the games would fit cosily in their programme schedules. Surely this is neither in the players' interests or the television companies. A few extra minutes of excitement with one team going all out for an equalizing goal would be better entertainment and boost viewing figures far more than players feigning injury or walking at funeral pace to take a throw-in and then leaving it for a colleague from even further away and walking at an even slower pace.

Three of the quarter-final games were settled on penalties, which is a harsh way to go out of the competition. There can't be many people who relish the responsibility of taking a penalty in front of all those fans and the millions watching on television especially with so much at stake. The pressure must be enormous and I was glad not to be one of the five assigned to take them for England.

If a game ends in a draw the best way to decide the result is to replay. But with the tight scheduling of the World Cup and the physical demands it would place on the players that probably isn't possible. One suggestion is that the game should continue until one team scores. I don't think that is a satisfactory solution and there's the possibility that some games, like Mexico against West Germany, could go on for hours.

You shouldn't really miss a penalty; a free shot from twelve yards. Unless the keeper has a stroke of luck and guesses correctly then he shouldn't have a chance. A better finish would be the American style shoot-out, which is just as nerve wracking but adds that extra excitement. I've been involved in quite a few of those when Ipswich have toured the United States and it is a lot harder than it looks.

The idea is you start with the ball about twenty-five yards from goal with just the goalkeeper to beat and five seconds to do it in. The goalie can come off his line which adds to the excitement. Different players have contrasting ideas on how to score and some will chip the keeper while others try to go round him. It makes the odds that much more even as you have to beat the keeper and the clock. It's been a success in America where crowds would rather see the shoot-out than the normal ninety minutes, but it would be a brave man to introduce it into the World Cup especially now that penalties are established.

Some people feel the third and fourth place play-off should be scrapped, but I disagree. Having got so close to the final it gives you a chance to overcome the disappointment of losing a semi-final and offers you the chance to finish third in the world, which is no mean feat. With another game, you can go out and play free of the worries of being knocked out. France left out several stars this time but I would have loved to play – I just wished we had got that far.

Before the 1990 finals in Italy I hope FIFA review the way they pick referees. If a European team played a South American team they would appoint a Third World referee. The chances were he didn't understand the pace of the European game or the finesse of the South Americans and some of the decisions would be baffling to both sets of players.

Refereeing inconsistencies mean players don't know where they stand. In some games players would get away with wild tackles and body checks while other players were booked for petty offences causing no damage to an opponent.

Despite these criticisms, the World Cup is still the greatest competition in the world. I am honoured to have played in two and I hope I am still on the international scene when the next tournament comes around in 1990.

12

On the Move

The decision to leave Ipswich was one of the hardest of my life. It was not just a matter of where to go but whether to go. I had supported them as a boy, and as a player I had known success and failure but I still maintained a deep love for the club. I would be leaving my home and my friends and a happy way of life and moving into the unknown. And transfers are not always a success. I knew of several players who lived to regret the day they signed for a new club.

As the UEFA side started to break up there had inevitably been talk that I would join the queue of players waiting to leave Portman Road and the rumours were fuelled by constant press speculation. However, unlike the other players, I had signed a four year contract with Ipswich and, although they wanted to get away, I was happy to stay. As the club's League position became more serious, I felt there was no way that I could leave when they needed me – I would have felt like a deserter. Football fans were fed up with the attitude of some players who failed to show any loyalty to a club or to the fans who paid their wages and gave them a more than comfortable lifestyle.

So although I was flattered to read in the newspapers that clubs like Manchester United, Tottenham and Arsenal were interested I knew my loyalties lay with Ipswich. There was a short time early in 1985 when it looked as though the club was considering selling me. Ron Atkinson had once again said that he wanted me to stiffen the United defence and journalists phoned me at home and suggested the best places to live in the Manchester area. Ipswich were in debt and had young players like Ian Cranson ready to take my place. For a while, Rita and I thought that a move could be on the cards. Then I saw Bobby Ferguson and he confirmed that Ron Atkinson had made an offer, but said that whatever happened Ipswich would not sell me. That was fair enough. I had spent nine fantastic years at the club, had three years of my contract to run and I was happy to stay.

Rita and I had grown up in Suffolk, which is a lovely part of the country. Our families lived nearby, we had plenty of friends in the area and were a five minute drive from Portman Road. We had spent time renovating and redecorating our house which was just as we wanted it. Rita's father did most of the work. I am no DIY expert and useless with hammer and nails. We lived a nine iron from Bobby Robson's house and I often used to bump into him when we were walking our dogs. It was handy for me and I was able to remind him that I was still around when he was picking the England squad!

In the summer of 1985 Ipswich offered me an improved three-year contract which included a clause that they would release me if we were relegated. I never thought we would go down and was looking forward to a revival in our fortunes. Of course, it did not happen and at the end of the season we were relegated with Birmingham and West Brom.

The day after our relegation was confirmed I was due to leave for Mexico with the rest of the England squad for the World Cup. Before we left I went into the ground to see Bobby Ferguson. We talked in his office and went over the games we had lost and the points we had dropped during the season, which had led to our relegation. He agreed that I would be able to go if I wanted, but suggested that I wait until after the World Cup before I became involved in any talks. 'There will be all kinds of speculation,' he said. 'The best thing for everyone is for you to concentrate on doing well in the World Cup. We don't want your mind distracted by transfer worries. There will be plenty of time for that afterwards.'

Of course, there was no escape from the speculation. Journalists had already been phoning my home to ask about my future and the regional television cameras were at Ipswich that morning. While we were away in Mexico, Bryan Robson kept joking about how I would be his team-mate at Old Trafford the following season and the Spurs players, Glenn Hoddle, Chris Waddle and Gary Stevens were saying: 'Oh no he won't. He'll be at White Hart Lane.'

David Pleat had recently been appointed Tottenham manager and was in Mexico working with ITV Sport. He told me that he wanted to sign me and Mitchell Thomas from his old club Luton.

There had also been talk that Arsenal had renewed their interest, and Brian Clough apparently said that he would like me to play for Nottingham Forest which was very flattering.

My room-mate, Viv Anderson, christened our room the 'busy room' during the World Cup because of the number of phone calls I was receiving. I received one call from a journalist who said that Graeme Souness wanted to sign me for Glasgow Rangers. It came out of the blue and I was chuffed that a Scottish club apparently wanted to buy an Englishman. I explained that I wanted to concentrate on the World Cup before making a decision and that I was hoping to listen to other offers. I wanted to keep my options open.

With so many clubs supposedly interested I expected the move to be straightforward. I wanted to stay in the First Division. A move to Europe, which had been suggested, seemed unlikely to me. Their big clubs tend to spend money on players who either score goals or create them and not on defenders. Dave Watson, the former England centre-half, went to Werder Bremen in West Germany, but it was not a great success and he was back home within a year.

There was one week in the summer of 1985 when I thought I might get the chance to play abroad. I received a phone call from an agent in Belgium who said he was representing a big Italian club. They had seen me play for England against Romania in Bucharest and wanted to sign me. Would I be interested? I thought it was one of the lads messing about, but he phoned again and convinced me that it was genuine.

My mind started racing, and Rita and I could hardly contain our excitement at the thought of a lucrative move to Italy. Ray Wilkins and Trevor Francis had told me about their lifestyle since they had moved there and it seemed too good to be true.

The agent phoned again and said the club were still interested. He did not tell me which club it was but asked if I wanted to discuss terms. I said I would love to but it would be better for all of us if we followed the official procedure and he approached the Ipswich manager first. Rita and I spent the next few days studying maps of Italy and I really thought my boat had come in. I would have loved to play in Europe and widen my experience playing against a different style of football.

I phoned the England manager, Bobby Robson, and his advice was 'if you get the chance take it'. But nothing happened. I do not know whether Ipswich turned down the offer or if the Italian club lost interest, but the agent never phoned again and the issue faded away as mysteriously as it had arrived.

Once the World Cup was over, I still had hopes that I would be joining Manchester United. They had been interested for the last couple of seasons and I would have jumped at the chance of joining them. They are, after all, one of the biggest clubs in the world. I knew some of the players and the club had everything you wanted – big crowds, glamour and a great stadium.

I arrived home from Mexico and flew straight out of the country again, this time to Portugal where Rita and the boys were on holiday with my parents. Looking back it was probably the wrong time to go with so many loose ends that needed to be tied up at home, but the holiday was booked and we had all been looking forward to spending some time together after so long apart.

It was Portugal, of course, who beat England in our first game in the World Cup and I was surprised that the waiters in the restaurants recognized me. At one of the restaurants we received a free bottle of champagne from the owners with the message 'Compliments of Carlos Manuel' – the man who had scored for Portugal in that game. I was even invited to play in a football match out there with some of the Portuguese internationals, but after my last encounter with their team I decided against it.

While we were in Portugal I received a call from Chelsea who said they were interested. When we arrived home I drove down to Brentwood for a chat with their manager, John

Hollins. We talked generally for a while and I told him the kind of terms I was looking for. He gave me the impression that there would not be any great problem and said he would contact me again once he had spoken to his chairman. A week later he phoned and said he was still interested and I was beginning to think a move to Chelsea could be on. Then a couple of days later I opened a newspaper and saw that they had signed Steve Wicks from Queen's Park Rangers for £500,000. He is a similar sort of player to me and it seemed that they had changed their minds about buying me. I did not hear another word from Chelsea.

The new season was looming and my future was as uncertain as it had been when I had left for the World Cup finals. It was unsettling for my family. Christopher, my elder son, would be old enough to go to school in the following term but we did not know where we would be living. Reporters would phone up and say 'Any news?'

'No, nothing,' I would say.

'What? There must be some news.'

But there was not. There were plenty of rumours, but the truth was nobody seemed interested.

The £1 million that Ipswich were apparently looking for was a ridiculous figure and I didn't think I was worth that much. But having said that, I was disappointed that not one English First Division club made a firm bid for me. I had been linked with so many clubs over the past two years, but now I seemed to be the forgotten man. I had just come back from the World Cup finals where I thought I had done quite well, I was still only twenty-seven and I had a few more years in front of me. Rita and I thought we would be able to take our pick of the clubs, but as the days passed nothing happened. I was sure someone would phone and was scared to go out in case I missed them. But the wait indoors was all in vain.

It soon became apparent that Manchester United were not going to make a bid. Bryan Robson had phoned me at home and told me that he thought they were interested, but I heard later that the board decided not to buy me. The only call I received was from Graeme Souness who confirmed that he was keen to sign me for Rangers. He has a good line in sales talk and told me how Rangers could offer me European football with one of the biggest clubs in the country. 'With you in the side the club will do well and the fans will worship you like a god,' he said. As an Englishman I was very dubious about that! I had always thought the English League was the best in the world and didn't have a particularly high regard for Scottish football, probably because I didn't know very much about it. But Graeme was very persuasive and the more I spoke to him the more I changed my mind.

Then I received a phone call from a man who said he was from the children's charity UNICEF and that they were organizing a game in Pasadena to raise money for refugees from the Mexico City earthquake. He wanted me to play for Rest of the World team. I am very gullible and I was convinced it was one of the lads playing a joke, but when he assured me he was serious, I jumped at the chance. I knew I had not been the first choice, but it was still a wonderful honour.

I spoke to Bobby Ferguson and once he had sorted out my insurance he was happy for me to go. Two days later I was in a rush-hour crush on the London Underground on my way to Heathrow to catch my flight to Los Angeles. When I arrived in America the organizers met me in an enormous limousine with iced champagne in the bar, stereo and television – absolute luxury! I kept thinking: What am I doing here? It was such a contrast to my crushed journey on the Piccadilly Line in London.

The players were staying at the Sheraton Grand and I bumped into Brian Moore and Gerry Harrison, the ITV football commentators, and Michael Hart a journalist from the *London Evening Standard*. I was glad to see some friendly faces and they showed me the best places to enjoy a beer.

Our squad was managed by Franz Beckenbauer and included some of the best players in the world. Dasayev, the Russian goalkeeper, was there with his international team-mate Igor Belanov who scored some cracking goals in the World Cup. Soren Lerby was there from Denmark, Paulo Rossi from Italy, Amoros from France and Uli Steilike and Felix Magarth from West Germany. I kept wishing that I could speak a foreign language and we were communicating in broken English, bits of French and plenty of imaginative signs.

Training with such great players was a marvellous experience. Pat Jennings had been made captain of our team for his farewell game. Now he had reached the age of forty-one he also found the training quite exhausting and after one session Beckenbauer said: 'There will not be a shooting practice because Pat is tired.' So I volunteered to go in goal and try to save shots from some of the most lethal finishers in the world. I sympathize with goalkeepers and they earn every penny they receive. With players like Lerby, Belanov and Rossi firing in shots you have no time to think. I was wearing Pat's gloves, but my hands were stinging afterwards from the force of some of the shots.

It was also an eye-opener as far as learning how other players prepare for a big game. I was sitting near the Mexican World Cup players Nigrete and Sevin when we had lunch before a training session and couldn't believe my eyes as I saw them munch their way through chilli bean after chilli bean. My stomach would have exploded, but they didn't think anything of it.

As one of the few English speakers on the trip I found myself in demand for press, radio and television interviews. The game had captured the imagination of the American public and was due to be shown in more than seventy countries.

The morning of the game was quite smoggy with temperatures in the seventies which was comfortable for Pat, Gordon Strachan and myself. We were happy and looking forward to a game which wouldn't be too strenuous when the smog lifted, the temperature rocketed and it was like being in Mexico again.

After fifteen minutes we won a free-kick on the edge of their area. Gordon Strachan moved over to take it and signalled for me to push up. I knew roughly where Gordon would put the ball and as I attacked the space the cross came over perfectly for me to get in a firm header sending it past Pumpido in the America's goal. I was as surprised as the crowd who had come expecting to see Maradona score, not an unknown from Ipswich. But what a feeling to score against such quality opposition and with so many people watching. Paulo Rossi made it 2–0, volleying home a superb cross from Magarth who impressed me throughout the game. I don't think many of us had done much training since the World Cup finals which ended four weeks earlier and, as we tired, the Americas pulled back the two goals. Roberto Cabanas, the Paraguyan, scored the first and two minutes from time Maradona seized on a loose ball to poke home the equalizer.

That evening Pat, Gordon and I went out to sample the Los Angeles night-life. The famous divorce lawyer Marvin Mitchelson invited us to a party at his house, which was like something out of one of those glamorous films. It was pure tinseltown and a rare taste of Hollywood glitter for three ordinary Brits. From there we went on to a few bars and arrived back at the hotel at about three o'clock.

Three hours later the phone rang in my room. Graeme Souness was on the other end and said he wanted to meet me at a hotel near Heathrow as soon as I arrived back in England so he could persuade me to join Rangers. I think I was still drunk and incapable of any form of articulate reply, but I managed a couple of grunts before putting the phone down and going back to sleep.

Later that morning the Tottenham secretary, Peter Day, phoned and said Spurs were interested and wanted to meet me when I arrived back in England. I explained that I was meeting Graeme Souness first and we arranged to meet after I had spoken to him. At last things seemed to be moving.

I flew back with Gordon Strachan and when we arrived at Heathrow I made straight for the Holiday Inn where I thought I was supposed to meet Graeme. I waited and waited, but there was no sign of him. Meanwhile he was waiting at the Sheraton wondering what had happened to me. I had been so drowsy when he phoned that I had forgotten which hotel he had said and had now gone to the wrong one. Luckily I phoned Rita and she managed to sort things out with messages to Graeme via Rangers. He phoned me at the Holiday Inn reception and said: 'What on earth are you doing there? I said the Sheraton!' He told me not to move because he was coming straight round.

Graeme must have wondered what kind of idiot he was dealing with. I had been incoherent on the phone and now I couldn't even find the correct meeting place. But he was very charming and once again told me what a great club Rangers was and suggested that I come up to Ibrox to see for myself. I explained that I was due to see Tottenham that evening as Ipswich had accepted their bid. Graeme looked surprised.

'That's news to me,' he said. So he phoned Patrick Cobbold, the Ipswich chairman, who told him that Tottenham's bid was lower than Rangers' and had been rejected. Rangers were the only club with a bid that was acceptable and the only club that I could talk to.

I had been impressed with Graeme Souness who had done everything by the book and was straight with me from the start. So the meeting with Tottenham was cancelled and we flew to Scotland where Rangers hid me in a hotel outside Edinburgh where I was safely out of sight.

I had played at Ibrox in a pre-season friendly with Ipswich in 1981. The stadium was magnificent and you could appreciate the history and tradition of the club from seeing the impressive wood-panelled entrance hall and the trophy room packed full of cups, pennants and prizes. The lads had loved the changing rooms which were enormous. There were more than 25,000 fans at the game, which was a good crowd for a friendly and higher than our average for League games that season. We won 2–1, with John Wark scoring both our goals and Ally Dawson scoring for Rangers. Alan Brazil had always been a Celtic fan and was desperate to score against Rangers, but he was through twice and missed both times.

Rita came up to look around and, although it rained heavily all day and she saw Glasgow at its worst, she seemed quite keen to move to Scotland. I still had a few doubts at the time. I had been surprised when Chris Woods had joined Rangers from Norwich and it was an unusual step for an English player to move north of the border. But the more I saw of Rangers the more I could believe Graeme Souness when he said they were one of the biggest clubs in Europe.

The fans had been tremendous. Hundreds stopped me in the street and said they hoped that I would sign. I had a chat with Chris Woods and he told me that the club had been marvellous to him. I discussed terms with Graeme. He had to keep rushing out of the room to consult his chairman and I kept in touch with my accountant by phone. He said it was a good offer, but I asked Souness if I could sleep on it before giving my decision. I was still wondering if an English club had put in an increased offer, but when I phoned Ipswich they said that they hadn't received any new bids. Tottenham had been trying to reach me, but I couldn't talk to them unless Ipswich accepted their bid, and they didn't seem to be prepared to increase their offer.

I phoned Ipswich again the next day and Mr Cobbold again said that there had been no new offers. We chatted for a while about the old days and then he said: 'Well if Rangers are the club for you then you have our blessing. Good luck!'

I phoned David Pleat and told him that I was signing for Rangers. He asked me to wait for a day or two and was very persuasive in trying to get me to change my mind but it was too late. I had given my word to Graeme Souness.

I would have liked to play for Tottenham. They are a big club and with a new manager and players like Glenn Hoddle and Chris Waddle, they had a very good team. White Hart Lane is a great stadium and the people there have always been friendly to me, which I appreciate. Even after I signed for Rangers and went there for a pre-season friendly a few days later everyone made me feel welcome. There were a few wry comments about 'why didn't you sign for us', but everyone wished me luck in my new career at Rangers.

I had no doubts about the standard or quality of Scottish football. I knew how strong teams like Aberdeen were after playing them when I was with Ipswich and if it was good enough for Graeme Souness and Chris Woods it was good enough for me.

Our move to Scotland went very smoothly. After a week or two in a hotel, Rangers put us up in a club house in Helensburgh which meant we could start living as a family once more. Rita and I were obviously sad to leave our home in Ipswich, but everyone in Scotland made us feel welcome. We hadn't realized how passionate the Scots are about their football and on the day we moved the removal men, who were firm Rangers fans, were astonished to see Rita wearing green trousers. They made it very clear that it wasn't the done thing to wear such a colour if you had anything to do with Rangers.

I was still wary about how the Ibrox fans would react to my arrival. I shouldn't have worried. For my first game, a friendly against Bayern Munich, I was given a tremendous reception by a crowd of more than 36,000. It was the start of a new career and that welcome made me feel sure I had made the right move.

13

Close Encounters

Everybody loves a goalscorer except perhaps the poor defender who has to mark him. I have played against some of the greatest forwards in the world, and there's no doubt in my mind that Diego Maradona is the best of the lot. Anyone who saw his displays in the 1986 World Cup would probably agree that he's in a class of his own. But when it comes to goalscoring Ian Rush isn't far behind him. Give Ian half a chance and he's virtually guaranteed to score. He's quick, sharp and deadly with both feet. His finishing is of the highest order, but he's also good with his back to goal. He's so fast when he turns and he's able to peel off his marker so quickly that he causes all kinds of problems for defenders. I like a chat with my opponent during the game, but Ian is one of those forwards that is so wrapped up in the match that you can't get a word out of him. Off the pitch he loves a laugh and a joke but during a game he's very quiet.

When it comes to finishing there's not much to choose between Ian Rush and Gary Lineker. I remember playing against Gary in his early days with Leicester. He impressed us then with his pace and although he wasn't as deadly in front of goal in those days he still scored the winner against us at Filbert Street.

Gary is an unflappable character who takes everything in his stride. He is still as likeable and as modest as he was in his Leicester days, despite his million pound moves to Everton and Barcelona. Working with better players has helped to improve his game. At Everton he partnered Graham Sharp and had Trevor Steven, Kevin Sheedy, Peter Reid and Paul Bracewell in support. Such quality back up helped him to score thirty goals in forty-one League games in the 1985–86 season, which is a fantastic record. After his move to Barcelona he seemed to sharpen up even more, and his four goals for England against Spain in Madrid in February 1987 capped a marvellous performance. Over the years he has matured and become a more positive player with the confidence to take on and beat defenders with that sudden burst of speed. You can never rattle him. He's so calm and although he is often the victim of some quite brutal challenges he never seems to retaliate.

One of the first players I had to mark at the beginning of my career was Kenny Dalglish. Since then I've faced him regularly when he has played for both Liverpool and Scotland. He's always been a handful. Once the ball is played in to him it seems to stick. He holds it so well that defenders can't get in with a tackle. He also has a great eye for picking out runners and can play those precision passes into their path completely splitting open a defence.

Kenny is a great finisher and scored some tremendous goals. There was one at Portman Road where he cut in from the right, beat a couple of defenders and curled a left-foot shot inside the far post, which was typical Dalglish.

Kenny's also a crafty character. I remember him winning a penalty against Ipswich at Anfield in the 1980–81 season. It was a close game and the score was 1–1. Liverpool had a lot of the play but we were defending well and looked like holding on until Kenny, who had been backing into me, took a dive. I hadn't touched him but the referee was taken in and to my amazement he gave a penalty.

Justice was done in the end thanks to a trick from Frans Thijssen. As Terry McDermott came up to take the penalty Frans threw a wad of mud at the ball. I'm sure it put Terry off because he mishit his shot and Paul Cooper saved!

Playing against Kenny taught me a lot, and I soon learnt not to commit myself and dive in to a tackle inviting the forward to nip round you. After seeing Kenny get away a couple of times I started to steady myself and judge when to make the tackle.

Charlie Nicholas has a similar style to Kenny and is superb at holding the ball and then laying off some beautifully weighted passes for colleagues making a run. I've faced Charlie several times when he's played for Arsenal and Scotland and seen at close quarters his tremendous skill. I've tried to rattle him early on but you can't scare him. He's a great character and you can always have a good laugh with him during the game. He's a Celtic fanatic. I've met him a few times socially and we've had several discussions about Scottish football, although we disagree when it comes to choosing the best team in Glasgow!

I have always preferred marking a big, bustling centre-forward in the Joe Jordan mould. You know what to expect and that you will be in for a tough, physical battle. Joe was always aggressive and particularly dangerous on the far post where he was always a worry for defenders. They knew he was lurking somewhere behind them and they were always half expecting him to crash into them. Often they would take their minds, or their eye, off the ball for a split second and then WHACK! Either Joe would score or they would end up with another painful bruise. You had to be careful with Joe. He would often go quiet for periods during a game then there would be a crunch as he flew in for a challenge and you would end up with a tooth missing or a bloody nose. I used to try and talk to Joe during a game, but he was another player who was so wound up that you couldn't get a word from him.

Graham Sharp of Everton is a bit like Joe. He's always physical but has a lot of skill for a big man and lays off some great balls. He's quick, brave and fearless and gets in where the studs and boots are flying. He's one of the best Scottish strikers of his time and he's been an important part of Everton's success since he joined them from Dumbarton.

Cyrille Regis is one of the strongest players that I have ever faced. He's powerful and incredibly well built. He gave me a shoulder barge in one game which sent me flying. I eventually landed about fifteen yards away and felt as though I had bounced against a brick wall. Cyrille is very quick, and if he receives the right kind of pass he can beat any defence for speed. Defenders have to try and keep him with his back to goal otherwise he will cause all kinds of problems. If you can stop him running at you with the ball or running into space you have a chance to keep him quiet.

Although Cyrille is always likely to give his opponent a few bruises during the game, he is a very fair player and not the sort to swing his elbows or kick. It's a question of the stronger man winning on the day when you face Cyrille. I've known him since our days in the England Under-21 team and he's a great character. We always look forward to a couple of pints together after the game.

In Scotland Sandy Clark, the Hearts centre-forward, is a typical old-fashioned number nine, who is aggressive, hard and will always give you a tough game. You can never guarantee that you'll dominate him and if you win a header then he'll probably win the next. Hearts play to his strength and hit long, driven balls into him so he can flick them either side of his marker for runners to break on to. Other times he will take the ball on his chest and hold up the play while he waits for support. It's an effective system that Hearts have developed and, with runners like John Robertson and John Colquhoun alongside him and Gary Mackay and Neil Berry feeding off him in midfield, it's hard for defences to combat.

Ideally you need a player positioned in front of Sandy to cut out the balls directed at him, but at Rangers we can't afford that luxury because our midfield men are already engaged in their own roles.

Small forwards can cause big defenders problems. For instance, Steve Moran of Leicester has always given me a hard time. He's only five feet eight inches tall, about eight inches shorter than me, but he's very quick and takes up some great positions. He regularly scored against Ipswich. I often found myself in a one-against-one with Steve and there were several times when he used his pace to nip past me. When Southampton had Steve playing alongside Kevin Keegan they were a hard team to play against. Two short, stocky forwards who both had pace always caused problems when they turned a big defender.

I was delighted when Kevin Keegan retired as it meant that I wouldn't have to mark him again. He was built like a shorter version of Cyrille Regis with very muscular arms and legs. He jumped well for high balls and made it hard for a defender by leaning into them as he jumped. I trained with him for England

and noticed then what a fierce competitor he was and how hard he worked at his game, practising time and time again until he had perfected some new skill.

Paul Mariner is one forward who would definitely make my all time top team. I played alongside him for six seasons at Ipswich and against him a few times when he played for Arsenal. He was a great sight when he was in full flight and scored 135 goals in 339 games for Ipswich. He used to frighten the most hardened defenders with his aggression and he was always bustling and forcing them into mistakes. Bobby Ferguson used to say that Paul knitted the Ipswich side together when he was playing well. He's also a great pal off the pitch and used to come along to heavy metal concerts when we were both at Portman Road.

In one of my first games for Rangers I soon discovered that Paul Sturrock is one of the best strikers in Scotland. We were beating Dundee United 2–0 when 'Luggy', as the lads call him, took control and changed the game steering United to a 3–2 victory. He's much underrated in England and I'm surprised that he hasn't won more caps for Scotland. He is always looking for the ball, either to his feet where he shields it well and makes it hard for defenders to tackle, or over the top where he uses his powerful running to take on defenders.

Paul Sturrock is hard to mark because he's so elusive and wanders all over the pitch, and either gets away from his marker or pulls him out of position leaving a gap in the defence. I've sometimes thought that he could be even more effective if he had a big man alongside to feed off. He's another player who likes a laugh during a game and is always chatting to the man who's marking him.

Brian McClair and Mo Johnston have established a good goalscoring partnership with Celtic. McClair in particular causes problems for his opponents with his breaks from deep. He's quick with a good touch and his late runs make it hard for defences to pick him up. He creates a lot of chances for his colleagues and with someone as sharp as Mo Johnston around they are always likely to be dangerous. Mo is quick to seize on parries and ricochets and scores a large percentage of his goals from close range.

In England Tony Cottee and Frank McAvennie of West Ham

are another proven goalscoring partnership. Tony is very quiet and unassuming off the pitch, but during a game you can't afford to give him half a chance or he'll pop up with a goal. He works well with Frank, who takes a lot of knocks through a match. Coming from St Mirren, Frank knows a thing or two about the other side of football away from the glamour of a big city club like West Ham.

Clive Allen is another clinical striker. He's deceptive during a game when he looks almost casual at times, but as soon as there's a chance Clive pops up and scores. His close control is good and he's another of those players that always knows where the goal is.

Kerry Dixon has the same goalscoring knack. During the World Cup in Mexico he was known as 'Ernie' by the England boys because his haircut made him look like Ernie Wise! Whenever I have marked Kerry he has usually been quiet, leaving most of the talking to his old striking partner David Speedie. He's a character and will moan non-stop at his team-mates for most of the game and then suddenly start applauding them for a good ball. He gets up well for a little man and, like Kerry, Ian Rush and Clive Allen, he has that goalscorers' instinct. Some players always seem to be in the right place in the penalty-area and draw the ball like a magnet. I don't know whether it's fate or superb anticipation, but it's infuriating for a defender to mark someone tightly all game and then, when one ball breaks loose, see him nip in to score.

One of the best players I ever marked was Frank Worthington. He had so much skill and played with tremendous flare. In my early days with Ipswich, Frank was playing for Bolton and scored one of the best goals I have ever seen. It was at Burnden Park and Frank was on the edge of our area with his back to goal. We had a wall of defenders along our eighteen-yard line and there didn't seem to be any danger when Frank started juggling with the ball. I remember thinking: He's just trying to be flash, there's no problem here, when he flicked the ball over his head and over our defence and nipped round to volley home. It was unbelievable. The goal was regularly shown on television and was typical Frank. It's hard to believe that he only played for England eight times. A player with his skill and ability should have been a regular for many years.

Frank is always good for a laugh during a game. You soon get to know your opponents whether from international games, social functions or just playing against each other regularly. I always like to talk to the man I'm marking and ask how they are doing, how their family is and so on or share a moan about the pitch, the weather or the referee. A little chat can also serve another purpose in helping you gauge how you stand with your opponent psychologically. From what they say you can usually tell whether they are in the mood to play or not.

I have heard some centre-halves take it even further and say things to their opponent like: 'How much money are you earning?' Whatever the reply, the centre-half will then say: 'Is that all! Well so and so told me he's on double that and his team are down the bottom of the table.' If they are convincing enough they get their opponent more concerned about his wages than he is with what's happening in the game.

As captain you always have a chat with the opposing skipper when you go up for the toss. Some players appear quite relaxed while others are obviously very tense and it's normally nothing more than a quick 'hello' and 'all the best'. Before one game against Liverpool I was shaking hands with Phil Neal who was their captain at the time. I had just opened my insurance business in Ipswich and asked Phil if he had any insurance. I could see that he looked puzzled. Then I whipped out a calling card from the company and said: 'Give me a call if you need any – the phone number's on the card,' and ran back for the kick-off, leaving a bemused Phil standing on the centre-spot not knowing what to do with the card.

I like to have a laugh, but there are times when the talk can get quite nasty and often it can be X-certificate stuff. I've never had anyone come and threaten me, even in my naïve younger days. It may have something to do with my size, six feet four inches tall and fourteen and a bit stone. Forwards are often reluctant to say too much as they invariably have their back to the defender and realize you have a great chance of nobbling them if you want to.

Continental players often try to wind you up if you are British. In the Mexico World Cup some of the Portuguese team were rushing about and talking to us in broken English. They

would say things like 'Boo-cha, Boo-cha' and then come out
with a couple of swear-words that someone had taught them.
This was often accompanied by extraordinary hand gestures
which are obviously a great insult in their own country. It's
all quite ridiculous.

It even happened when Ipswich played a friendly in Iraq.
Their players were at it all game. Everyone seems to love to
have a go at the English, especially when we play abroad.
There are times when it can be hard not to react to the
provocation, but you've got to bite your tongue. As Graeme
Souness says: 'You've got to be cute. There's plenty of time to
have a go back.' If players are trying to wind you up it often
means that they are worried about you so, in a strange way,
they are paying you a compliment.

In my time at Ipswich I had two spells at left-back. Some
newspapers couldn't understand why a centre-half should play
there and for a time they suggested that it could cost me my
England place. But I'm convinced that the change helped to
improve my understanding of the game and made me a better
player. There's a lot of movement at full-back without seeing
much of the ball. You come inside to cover, push out to mark,
drop off to create space in front of you and then you're pushing
up on an overlap.

Initially I was worried about facing nippy little wingers, but
I soon realized that much of the game is a battle of wits against
your opponent. It was important to stop the winger running
at me so I would push up tight to get in with an early challenge.
If the winger had the ball I would force him wide. If he beat
me then at least he would be heading towards the corner flag
and away from danger. With central defenders like Russell
Osman, Kevin Beattie, Allan Hunter and Ian Cranson at the
back I was confident that our defence could cope with most
crosses.

Since those days I have been converted to a different theory
about full-back play where you try to force the winger inside
all the time. When he goes wide the midfield man covering
the full-back has to come behind and make up extra ground
towards the corner flag to cut him off. If the winger is forced
inside you are directing him to the man who is covering. If the
defence pushes up, not only have you blocked the winger's

space, but if he knocks it forward you've probably caught one or two players off-side. It's a good system and saves a lot of running for the midfield players. It's something that Liverpool have done for years and you rarely see them concede goals from crosses pulled back from the by-line.

The worst type of cross for defenders is the early ball, whipped low across the penalty-area behind the sweeper and in front of the goalkeeper. Big defenders will always feel confident about high crosses, but the low ball, hit with pace into that danger area, will always cause problems. It worked well for England in the 1986 World Cup and brought Gary Lineker two of his three goals against Poland. The crosses, from Everton's Gary Stevens and Steve Hodge, were hit early. The defenders can't play it for fear of touching it past their keeper for an own goal. It's important to hit the cross early. Too often you see players in that position with the opportunity to cross and instead they will try to beat their man or take the ball to the by-line and waste the chance.

The ball over the top will also cause defenders problems. Centre-halves are often big, cumbersome figures who don't have a great deal of immediate pace. Once they've turned it's hard to get both feet into the right position to get into a quick stride, especially when you're up against a nippy forward. In those instances defenders tend to drop off and leave a space in front rather than behind. At higher levels forwards can play a quick one-two and they'll have the pace to beat you again unless you can read the move and get into a position to stop the runs and cut out the return pass.

When the footballing awards are presented at the end of the season they normally go to goalscorers, occasionally to midfield players and goalkeepers, but hardly ever to a defender. Yet there are some great players in those positions, and not many are better than Alan Hansen, who has been so important in Liverpool's success story. He's not a dirty or physical player but he reads the game so well. That's an important part of a defender's game and can compensate for other deficiencies. Bobby Moore was quite slow, but he made up for that with the way he read the game and knew where the ball would go. Alan Hansen is quick for a big man and once he's won the ball he uses it well. His distribution is good and he always looks comfortable on the ball coming forward.

My ideal defender would have the pace, power and strength in the air of Kevin Beattie, the ability to read a game like Alan Hansen, be two-footed like Russell Osman and have the raw aggression of Graham Roberts. Graham's will to win frightens some forwards, but he's not a dirty player. A good defender knows when to go in for the ball and when to hold off. Kevin Beattie used to go in for tackles that he never had a chance of winning. The forward would knock the ball past him but Kevin could get away with it because he had the pace and ability to recover and win the ball in a second challenge. Poor labourers like myself haven't got that pace and we have to judge our first tackle more carefully.

I'm not a dirty player and I wouldn't even say that I am a hard player, but I do play to win and I will always compete for the ball. Defending is not always meant to be a pretty game. It's often tough and physical and the finesse only comes once you've won the ball. When I am tackling I always go for the ball and if a man gets in the way then that's too bad. When you challenge you can't afford to be second best. I'll make no excuses for the fact that I've kicked a few people in my time and I've been kicked by a few people as well, but that's the way of football.

I soon found out that you can't go into a game as a professional thinking that you won't end up with a few cuts and bruises. When I'm marking a player I have to think that it's either him or me. I know that it's a mercenary attitude, but the centre-forward will take money out of your pocket if he scores. Obviously you don't kick him to bits, but it's important to beat him.

The fans at Ipswich and Rangers have always been good to me, but I get a lot of stick from crowds when we play away. I've always had a bad time at Nottingham Forest where I've been constantly heckled and spat at by some fans. It's not necessarily the youngsters and teenagers that are to blame and often the worst offenders are middle-aged or elderly men. They seem to get so wound up with their football and start to think that I'm some kind of animal. A 'donkey' is their favourite expression.

At small grounds like Southampton's you are close to the

crowd and even more aware of what's being said. There's one section at the Dell that always picks on one of the opposing players and when Ipswich played there it was always me. It would be Terry Butcher this and Terry Butcher is a so and so, all game. It can create an intimidating atmosphere and I shouldn't think that European sides enjoyed playing there.

Luton is another small ground with a hostile section of supporters. After my terrifying experience there in 1982, when I broke my nose and nearly died after losing so much blood, I've been the object of some sick chants. For the next four years whenever I played there the crowd would sing 'Butcher, Butcher break your nose', which they thought was a great joke.

As an Englishman and an expensive signing I receive a lot of stick in Scotland and I'm quite used to chants about Maradona, Argentina and being a waste of money! But down south I could never understand the hostility from crowds. I used to enjoy going to Liverpool, but I made a couple of mistakes in one game and the fans in the Kop slaughtered me. In the questionnaires sent round by football magazines I always used to say that the friendliest away fans were at Liverpool but not any more!

It's always baffled me why supporters should be so hostile. On a Wednesday I would play for England and have the entire country behind me and then a few days later I would play for Ipswich away from home and have the crowd calling me all the names under the sun. One minute they love you, the next thing you're treated like something that's crawled out from under a stone.

I'm sure that crowds can sometimes influence match officials, especially at intimidating grounds like the Dell where the fans are close to the pitch. It takes a brave man to defy the persuasion and provocation of thousands of screaming voices just a few feet away and I'm sure there are times when a flag has stayed down under pressure from the crowd.

It's not easy being a linesman and even from my limited experience running the line in junior games I've come across some of the problems. It's not a job that I would fancy.

I was once in favour of ex-professional players becoming referees, but I've since changed my mind. Although they would

have a good knowledge of the game, I think they would never
be able to escape their past allegiances from their playing days.
No matter how hard they try there will always be supporters
who remember what happened in the past and what they did
when they came to their ground as a player and it could make
it impossible for them to referee properly.

I've had my disagreements with referees over the years and,
although I'm convinced that the best refs in the world are here
in Britain, we've still got a few bad ones. Some whistle at
anything and break the game's rhythm with constant inter-
ruptions while others let too much go and lose control. Arrogant referees are unpopular with players. There are a few
referees who make an extraordinary scene about having a few
words with a player. For example, they'll stand firm and make
the player walk fifteen or twenty yards towards them. That
gets the player's back up and often annoys the crowd as well.

Good referees use their common sense. They let players
know that they are in charge and try and diffuse any hint of
trouble before it breaks out. A quiet word in a player's ear as
they run past is more effective than an arrogant lecture, and
it lets the player know that they won't be able to get away
with any nonsense.

My favourite referee was Alf Grey. He comes from Gorleston,
just up the coast from my home town, Lowestoft. He's retired
now but still works as an assessor and often covers games at
Portman Road. He used to despair at some of my performances.
I get worked up during a game and I'm not always shy about
telling a referee that I disagree with his decision. Alf has often
given me a lecture after a game. 'What were you playing at?'
he would say. 'It was obvious you were going to be booked.
When are you going to learn not to have a go back at referees?'

I know that I'm in the wrong but football is an emotional
game. One bad decision can be the difference between success
and failure. The referee can go back to his job as a surveyor
or newsagent or whatever the next day, but footballers depend
on their success on the field for their living. Sooner or later the
day has got to come when we have full-time referees.

14

Ibrox Skolars

Before I joined Rangers the trophy cabinet in our living room was rather bare – only one medal in my ten years as a professional footballer, that for the UEFA Cup Final in 1981. But within ten months of moving to Glasgow my collection had trebled with Rangers winning the Skol Cup and then the Scottish League title. Graeme Souness had told me he wanted Rangers to be the best team in Britain, but I don't think either of us expected such success to come so quickly.

In fact, my first season at Rangers had contained more than its fair share of ups and downs. Within a week of the start of the season we had been written off as championship contenders after losing two of our first three games. The joy of winning the Skol Cup was soon forgotten when we crashed out of the Scottish Cup, losing that disastrous game at home to Hamilton Academical. And then we had an exciting run in the UEFA Cup, ending in controversy in Germany. Combined with my new lifestyle off the pitch, my introduction to Scotland was certainly eventful and it seemed as though something dramatic happened every week.

Rangers had surprised everybody by signing three players from England for the start of the 1986–87 season. Colin West, a bustling centre-forward, 6′ 2″ tall and nearly 14 stone, had joined them from Watford where his record included a goal in every other game. Chris Woods, an England international goalkeeper, had signed from Norwich City, where he had made more than 200 League appearances and built a reputation as one of the best keepers in the country. Now I had taken the road to Glasgow. The club had spent heavily and were obviously hoping that the investment would pay off.

Before a ball had been kicked there were people saying that the championship was already ours. The players and staff at Ibrox knew that it wouldn't be that easy.

Our first League game was away to Hibernian. The squad stayed together in a hotel on the Friday night and we woke up to a beautiful, hot, sunny August day. Everyone was excited. It was the start of a new season and the beginning of a new chapter in the history of Rangers Football Club. We all knew it was important to start well.

The drive from Glasgow to Edinburgh was amazing. The motorway was packed with coachloads of Rangers fans and it was obvious that our supporters were going to turn out in force. As we approached the Hibs ground the streets were alive with fans in Rangers colours creating a carnival atmosphere. It was like a Cup Final.

The Easter Road changing rooms were basic compared to those you find in the English First Division, but the atmosphere inside the ground was building up and when we went out to warm up, the Hibs fans were in full voice with a succession of derisory songs. Most were directed against the English players, and not for the last time that season did I have to listen to chants about 'Argentina' and 'Maradona'.

At the other end of the ground the Rangers fans were in good heart and gave us a rousing reception. I thought we started the game well, knocking the ball around confidently and building a couple of useful moves. But the first thing to hit me was the pace of the game. In England I had been used to having time to settle on the ball, but the Hibs players were quick to shut us down and were making their presence felt with some aggressive tackling.

The pace was unrelenting and the ball was being pumped from end to end. After about fifteen minutes Hibs played yet another long ball over our defence. As I ran back I thought I had it but Steve Cowan, the Hibs forward, nipped in to rob me. He hit a simple square pass for Stuart Beedie to score and give Hibs the lead. We were stunned. Our fans were silent. After all the publicity before the game about the new look Rangers, no one could believe that we had conceded a soft goal like that.

But almost immediately Ally McCoist put us level from the penalty-spot after he was fouled. The tackles were getting fiercer and then, eight minutes before half-time, the game erupted when our player-manager, Graeme Souness, took a kick at George McCluskey, the Hibs forward. There was pandemonium. All the players, except the Hibs keeper Alan Rough, were involved in the argument in the centre-circle. I had to restrain Chris Woods who had rushed from his goal to join the mêlée. A few minutes earlier he'd been elbowed in the face by McCluskey. Chris is normally mild mannered, but he was so angry at what was going on that I had to put him in a half-nelson to drag him away. McCluskey was carried off; Souness was sent off; and all twenty-two players, except Alan Rough, were later given two disciplinary points for their behaviour.

I wasn't surprised that the game exploded in the way it did. Everyone was so wound up that something was bound to happen. Hibs were playing like men possessed. You could see from the look in their eyes and the way they approached the game that they were treating it like a battle, Scots v. English, as if to say, 'We'll show those flash so-and-so's from Rangers with their big names and expensive signings that we're as good as them.' It was bound to lead to trouble. I'm not condoning what the gaffer did. He was wrong and has admitted it.

Temperatures were still running high when Steve Cowan put Hibs back in the lead, and before we had chance to fight back, the whistle went for half-time. Walter Smith took our team talk, trying to calm us down and make sure no one else did anything daft and got sent off. He kept saying that if we kept our heads and started playing the kind of football we knew we were capable of, the game was ours. The gaffer was too choked to say anything, and no one had the courage to ask him how he felt.

Our ten men played some good football and we pressed and probed without being able to score the vital goal. I was booked after swinging at Cowan with my elbow. He ducked and I missed. It was an act of frustration on my part. Cowan had come in with a rugby tackle as I went to clear the ball. It was the kind of thing that had been going on all game, and was the final straw as far as I was concerned.

What should have been a bright start to my new career had turned rather sour. I felt gutted, and in the calm of the changing room I wondered whether I had done the right thing in moving to Scotland. As I slowly untied my boots all kinds of thoughts went through my mind such as: Is it going to be a flop? and: Will the fans turn on us? But the supporters had been tremendous and gave us a great reception after the game. They still seemed optimistic.

Woodsy, Colin West, the gaffer and myself had all been playing our first League game in Scotland. The gaffer was born in Edinburgh but he had never played in Scottish football before, spending his career in England and Italy. The team was new and it would take time for us to get used to playing alongside each other.

Our first chance to make up for the defeat against Hibs came the following Wednesday, at home to Falkirk. But we didn't play well and scrambled to a 1–0 victory thanks to another penalty from Ally McCoist. I was happy to have notched my first Premier League victory, but playing for Rangers is similar to playing for England where you not only have to win but you have to play well. The Ibrox fans have long memories and have seen so many good sides at the club over the years that they have become used to high standards. We knew our performance hadn't been good enough.

The following Saturday we were at home to Dundee United, who'd been Scottish League champions in 1983 and had finished in the top three in each of the last four seasons. Walter Smith had been their assistant manager before moving to a similar position at Ibrox, so we knew a lot about them. Once again the fans turned out in force with more than 44,000 people inside Ibrox creating a fantastic atmosphere.

At last we turned it on and our first-half performance was one of our best of the season. We ripped them apart and went in with a 2–0 lead at the interval, receiving a tremendous ovation from the Rangers fans. We started the second half well but missed a couple of chances to put the result beyond doubt. Inexplicably we took our foot off the pedal and let United back into the game. With twenty minutes to go Kevin Gallacher nipped between me and Stuart Munro to make it 2–1. Then United scored twice in the last six minutes through Gallacher again and Ian Redford and we ended up losing 3–2. The half-time cheers turned to jeers by the end. We couldn't believe it. All three United goals were soft and the sort that we should never give away.

The manager was wild. 'How on earth can we expect to do anything this season if we let in goals like that!' he said and had a go at each of us in turn. We'd managed to turn a match-winning lead into defeat and deserved the roasting.

I believe that losing to Dundee United in the way that we did was the most important result of the season for Rangers. That may sound ridiculous, but when I look back that game stands out as the critical point of the season. It left us with two points out of a possible six from our first three games and we were already being written off as championship contenders. That lifted the pressure from the players for a start. We knew we would get better. The Dundee United game was only the fourth time we had played together as a team and we were still learning about each other. But more importantly that game taught us a lesson, that you should never let up when you're ahead, and we took note of it. For the rest of the season we were determined that once we'd gained control of a game we weren't going to throw it away again.

That was long term. In the short term we needed a good win under our belts. We had the chance the following Wednesday against Stenhousemuir in the Skol Cup. We won 4–1 and followed that with a 2–1 win over Hamilton in the League before meeting East Fife in the third round of the Skol Cup.

I had no idea where East Fife played and I wasn't much wiser when the lads explained that their ground was at Methil on the Fife coast. Every away trip was an adventure for me and the trip to East Fife was no exception. We arrived after a long drive from Glasgow and found a windswept ground right on the coast. It was cold enough in late August and I shivered as I imagined playing there in midwinter. The pitch, bumpy and sloped, was in a terrible condition after a long dry spell.

With respect to East Fife, it was like being drawn against a Southern League team in England. The changing rooms were cramped and only one wall had hooks on which to hang our clothes. With all thirteen players trying to get changed, it was impossible to pull on a shirt without poking someone in the eye and there was no room to tie a bootlace.

Walter Smith had seen East Fife play and warned us that their style was similar to Watford's. They get the ball forward early, with four up front and only two in midfield. The keeper never threw the ball out and always pumped long kicks forward. By now I was used to the more frenetic pace of the game in Scotland. Teams start off at 100 miles per hour and we'd learnt that if we matched them for the first thirty minutes or so the pace would drop and we could then start to knock the ball about in a more controlled style. In the first fifteen minutes we suffered a blow when Colin West went off with a ligament injury that was to keep him out of football for several months. In the second half we took control and bombarded their goal but couldn't score.

Ally McCoist missed a penalty and I hit the post, but as the game went into extra-time the prospect loomed that with all our expensive signings we could be dumped out of the cup by a First Division side. In those situations one piece of luck or a bad decision by the referee can decide a game, but after the extra thirty minutes there was still no score and we went to penalties.

Normally I keep out of the way at this time and I certainly never volunteer to take one, being much happier to let someone else shoulder the responsibility. But I realized that the lads were looking towards me and it struck me that as captain I was expected to take one. I was terrified, but I knew I couldn't let it show. I kept telling myself that I owed it to the team to be confident and bold. 'I'll take one,' I said, hoping that it wouldn't be necessary. 'You go third then,' said the gaffer, and as my stomach started turning I kicked myself for not having thought to nominate five others for the job before the game.

Ally McCoist and Ted McMinn scored for us to make it 2–2 before Chris Woods saved East Fife's third penalty. The pressure was really on now and as I walked up to the spot I kept thinking: What a terrible start to my career at Rangers if I miss and we go out of the cup. I placed the ball and decided to hit it as hard as I could, but as I came up I saw the goalkeeper move to his left. He was already committed so I just trickled the ball into the right. It wasn't the best penalty in the world but it gave us the lead. I'd never felt so relieved. Ian Durrant and Davie Cooper stepped up to score from their kicks and we were through. It had been a scramble but games like that are always difficult with the favourites there to be shot down by the smaller clubs.

We realized that we were now only one game away from the semi-final. Our opponents in the next round were Dundee. Since joining Rangers I'd heard all kinds of stories, legends and myths from people at the club, and one of the most popular superstitions was that Dundee were our bogey team. 'We never do well against them,' they used to say gloomily. It was all new to me and such stories didn't really mean a lot, but I could see that others took them seriously.

Once again there was a big crowd and a superb atmosphere at Ibrox. After twenty minutes Dundee were down to ten men since Jim Smith was sent off for a couple of fouls on Ted McMinn. We had all the play but couldn't score until midway through the second half when I knocked the ball out to Cammy Fraser who hit a marvellous shot to give us the lead. Cammy was a superb striker of the ball and everyone at Rangers was sad when he had to retire from the game with a pelvic injury later in the season.

We looked certainties for the semi-finals until, with only seconds to go, Dundee equalized with a goal we gave away after some poor defending. I could hear people in the stand saying: 'Oh no! Here we go again. Dundee the bogey team, and Rangers throwing it away.' But in the second period of extra-time we tore them apart and goals from Graeme Souness and Ted McMinn saw us through, and did a bit to kill the Dundee myth.

In the semi-final we met Dundee United. They were still cock-a-hoop from their 3–2 win at Ibrox in the League in August, but another story started doing the rounds saying Dundee United had a Hampden hoodoo. Apparently they never played well there, especially against Rangers.

Both semi-finals were at Hampden and on the Tuesday, Celtic beat Motherwell on penalties. We were cursing the fact that Motherwell hadn't beaten our old rivals, but there was the prospect of an Old Firm final if we could beat United. That was incentive enough for us.

We played well that night. Ally McCoist celebrated his birthday with our first goal and Ted McMinn scored our second after a typical solo run. After letting a two-goal lead slip in our first meeting with United in the League, we were determined there would be no repeat this time and, although they pulled a goal back in the last few minutes, we were able to hold on for a place in the final. I'd suffered the pain and misery of losing in semi-finals with Ipswich and know only too well the empty feeling there is inside you when that happens. Now I was on the winning side I was determined to make the most of it. It was a great reward for our fans who had been so patient during the first few games when things hadn't gone as well as they had expected. We'd repaid that loyalty by reaching a final.

I found it hard to believe that things had gone so well for me. Our League form had picked up and now I was in a cup final two months after signing for Rangers. Life was looking grand. The club had provided us with a house in Helensburgh while we looked for somewhere to buy. The people in Helensburgh had made us very welcome, and Chris Woods lived a couple of doors away so we were never lonely. We had a lovely view over the Firth of Clyde and each day on the way to training I drove past Loch Lomond. The view was so breathtaking that on one journey I nearly crashed the car off the road.

My main worries about moving to Glasgow had soon been dispelled. I had wondered whether the Scottish lads would resent an Englishman coming in as captain of their team, but they had gone out of their way to make me feel welcome. I enjoyed training and was impressed with the level of skill. Some of Davie Cooper's tricks, in particular, left me open mouthed in admiration.

The Rangers fans were marvellous and within a week one group had even named a branch of the supporters' club after me.

I was astonished at the size of the support for Rangers. Fans came to games from all parts of Scotland. Others came over on ferries from Northern Ireland and coachloads and carloads came up from Rangers supporters' clubs all over England. There's an excellent weekly magazine for supporters called *Rangers News* and copies are sent to fans all over the world. The club means so much to so many people and they are incredibly passionate about it.

I had played in my first 'Old Firm' game within a few weeks of joining Rangers. Everyone in England has heard about the Rangers v. Celtic games and the sense of occasion that surrounds the fixture, but when I walked out on to the Ibrox pitch I was amazed at the atmosphere. The Rangers fans had been loud for other games but for the Old Firm game the noise was phenomenal. For the Rangers players it's the most important match of the season. Most of our team have been Rangers supporters since they were boys, and lads like Ian Durrant and Derek Ferguson are really wound-up for days before the game.

We won that first match, Ian Durrant scoring the only goal, and it was as if we had won the League. The fans were going berserk. It didn't matter that we were in sixth place behind teams like Dundee and only one point ahead of Clydebank. Now we were to meet Celtic in the final of the Skol Cup at Hampden Park.

The final was played on a Sunday. Three days earlier we had played Boavista of Portugal in the UEFA Cup at Ibrox, coming back from a goal down to win 2–1. The game had been put back to the Thursday because Celtic were at home to Dynamo Kiev in the European Cup on the Wednesday. The authorities decided that Glasgow couldn't host two European ties on the same evening, so Celtic's match took priority, being the senior competition.

The win against Boavista was an important boost to morale and the lads went back to our hotel for a few beers that night. I think it is important for teams to have a few nights out from time to time. I'm convinced it helps to gel a side together and it's important for team spirit. The following day we were off to Troon where we stayed in the build up to the Skol Cup final.

I had stayed there with England, so I felt at home and we had a relaxed few days out of the public eye and away from the pressures which were obviously building up in Glasgow. I knew that luck was with us when I won on the horses on Saturday afternoon. I rarely bet, but we had nothing else to do after training except watch Grandstand and I picked a 16–1 outsider which came in easily.

Graeme Souness had been injured and there was speculation in the newspapers about whether he would be fit. The lads all

knew that he had no chance of playing, which was obviously
a blow for us. He's a great player and his big match experience
would obviously have been a steadying influence on some of
the younger players.

There was no training on the morning of the game so Davie
Cooper, Ted McMinn and I went for a stroll along the beach.
The bracing wind and the fresh sea air seemed a thousand
miles from the frenetic atmosphere of a packed Hampden Park.
It was my first domestic cup final and I still found it hard to
believe that I would be playing. After a light lunch we set off
for Glasgow. It was a route I knew well from trips with England
where I was used to crowds lining the streets to shout all kinds
of abuse at us. But this time the crowds cheered us all the way,
and as we approached Hampden Park there seemed to be a
mass of Rangers fans whichever way you looked.

At the time Celtic were three points ahead at the top of
the League and with Souness injured and Dave McPherson
suspended we were the underdogs. I had to do some pre-match
interviews on the pitch for radio and television along with the
Celtic skipper Roy Aitken, who's a smashing chap, but on this
occasion he seemed over confident. In fact, all the Celtic players
were swaggering around. When I got back to our dressing
room I was fired up and kept saying: 'Come on, lads. This lot
are too cocky. Let's take them down a peg or two.'

The atmosphere at Hampden was electric, and when we
walked out before the kick-off the noise that greeted both teams
was deafening. My mind was so concentrated on the game
that when the dignitaries came to be introduced to the players
I couldn't remember the names of my own team-mates and
fluffed my lines completely. I kept thinking: What a start to a
cup final! Players generally don't enjoy that part of the pre-
match build up. It adds to the tension and it's always a relief
when we break away and can kick a few balls around. The
small talk and long wait certainly isn't for the player's benefit –
we just want to get on with the game.

Perhaps Celtic were the better side on the day, but it's hard
to say. They certainly started well, although I managed to get
in an early tackle on Alan McInally, which settled my nerves.
Both sides had early chances, Cammy Fraser hitting the post
for us and then Mo Johnston was sent clear after a through

ball from Roy Aitken but he too hit the woodwork. There was a spell in the second half when we couldn't get the ball out of our half. Then all of a sudden our game clicked. Chris Woods had been superb from the start and at last the rest of us began to play.

Our first goal came from a free-kick. Derek Ferguson's cross just grazed my hair and Ian Durrant, who was lurking on the far post, controlled it beautifully on his chest and struck a left-foot shot past Pat Bonner. What a noise! We were playing towards the Rangers end and it seemed as though everyone had gone bananas. I would have been happy for the game to end right then.

But Celtic came back and Brian McClair scored a terrific goal to level the score. I remember thinking: That's it. We've blown it. But instead of tightening their grip, Celtic seemed to relax and give us the chance to pick ourselves up and fight our way back into the game once more. With six minutes to go we scored the winner. It came from another free-kick hit deep into the Celtic penalty-area. I knew I had the beating of my marker, Roy Aitken, and was about to pick my spot when I was pulled to the ground. It was a definite penalty.

I couldn't watch as Davie Cooper took it and instead kept my eyes fixed on the Celtic fans behind our goal. Nobody there moved. I was just aware of a tremendous noise from the Rangers fans at the other end signalling that we had scored. I turned round to see Davie waving his arms about, held aloft by Ally McCoist.

We expected Celtic to bombard us for the last few minutes, but the game was marred by Mo Johnston's sending off for butting Stuart Munro. It was a stupid thing to do and did nothing to help his team's cause as they needed him on the pitch.

I think we knew then that we'd won. After so many disappointments with Ipswich it was a tremendous feeling to be on the winning side and pick up a medal. I was interviewed on television and asked the normal question: 'How do you feel?' At a time like that it's hard not to reply with a cliché. You are so overcome by the moment and struck by a feeling of inner contentment and satisfaction at having achieved an ambition, that it's difficult to find words to describe your emotions.

I was so excited that someone had to show me where to go to receive the cups. There are two, the Skol and the League, but I couldn't see them and had to be guided by a policeman.

On the coach back to Ibrox it's a tradition for the captain to sit at the front next to the driver, displaying the cup for the fans on the route home. Thousands came out to give us a cheer. I could see how important it was to the supporters and I'm sure the celebrations lasted long into the night.

They certainly did for the players. After a reception at Ibrox we all went off to a night-club. I tried to take the League Cup with us, but Souness caught sight of me as I was going through the door. 'Where do you think you're going with that?' he boomed.

'I'm taking it with us to Panama Jacks?' I said.

'Oh no you're not. That stays here.'

It was a crazy night. Dougall, the club groundsman, slept with the Skol Cup to make sure it didn't disappear. Ally McCoist was up on a table to treat us to one of his famous five minute raps and the night ended for me when I fell asleep in the back of Chris Woods' car on the way home.

It was our first taste of success and we were hungry for more.

15

Champions of Scotland

There are so many factors involved in Rangers' success during my first season with the club, but the key to it all has to be Graeme Souness. In his first season as manager he transformed Rangers from a mid-table team to League champions. He restored the club's pride and revived public interest with more than a million people watching games at Ibrox during the season and nearly every away game sold out.

Graeme's influence was everywhere, both on and off the pitch. He impressed me in training where he dictated the pace of practice matches the way he does a real game. He's always able to calm things down, but at the same time he's aggressive and arrogant on the ball. He's got so much skill that he's got something to be arrogant about. He's a great reader of the game and seems to know what other players are going to do before they've made up their mind. His passing is first class, using the long ball well and also bringing players into the game. But what impressed me most was his attitude. He wanted to bring the best out in people. He's a winner and will accept nothing but the best from his players. It didn't take long to see why he had so much success with Liverpool and in Italy.

Graeme made some shrewd appointments. Walter Smith, the assistant manager, has a thorough knowledge of Scottish and international football. He's the quiet man of the partnership, but his advice is always precise and to the point. He's the opposite of Graeme who is prone to outbursts of temper when things go badly. The gaffer has knocked containers of orange squash flying, brought a television set crashing to the floor and damaged several dressing-room doors in the heat of the moment! Walter prefers the quiet approach and talks to players individually. They are a good team and work well together.

They also have good back-up from Peter McCloy who runs the reserve team and is still a useful keeper in training. Phil Boersma, who's a former team-mate of Graeme's, was appointed physio-coach and his voice is always booming out from the sidelines during the game. But team selection is always decided by Graeme and Walter. They always listen to players comments and suggestions and regularly ask for our opinions, but make their own minds up about picking the team.

On the pitch the boss tried to make us stamp our authority on the game early on, much in the way that Liverpool have done over the years. His team talks are short, sharp and to the point. They last only two or three minutes and concentrate on making sure that everyone is in the right frame of mind. Attitude is the key word. 'If you're attitude is right then you'll be OK,' he says. If we play a team from the bottom half of the table he'll point out that the game is set up for us to fall flat on our faces. 'Just make sure it doesn't happen,' he says.

Moving to Scotland had been a gamble for all the newcomers. Souness, like the Anglos, had never played in the Scottish Premier Division and we were playing at grounds we'd never seen before and against players we'd never met. In England I had become familiar with the vast majority of forwards in the First Division and I knew what they were likely to do, but in Scotland every game I was facing new players with different tricks and skills. Many of the teams were just names from the pools coupon and I had no idea where their grounds were. I was never able to tell Rita what time to expect me home from an away game as I never knew how far we were travelling, or how long it would take.

In fact, most of the grounds are quite close to Glasgow and I do much less travelling than I did in England. At Ipswich we'd regularly have a three-hour coach journey for an away game and would often travel Friday and stay overnight for a Saturday game. With Rangers the only overnight stay is when we play at Aberdeen, which is about two and a half hours away from Glasgow. Dundee takes just under two hours, but as Woodsy and I live in Bridge of Allan which is half-way there, the Ranger's coach picks us up and drops us off.

With the exception of Ibrox, Scottish grounds aren't as good as those in the English First Division. Even the top clubs, like Aberdeen, Hearts, Hibs, Dundee United and Celtic, lack the comfort you find at Highbury, Goodison, Old Trafford and White Hart Lane, where facilities are excellent. English clubs look after the players' interests with large comfortable changing rooms and spacious baths with room to stretch out and relax. I've been surprised at the number of dirty, dingy changing rooms I've come across in Scotland. Most are shabby with broken windows, tiles missing from the bath area and paint flaking off the walls. Obviously clubs in Scotland have smaller crowds, with teams like St Mirren and Dundee attracting fewer than 4,000 most weeks, so they can't afford to plough the money back into the ground in the way the big English teams like Spurs and Arsenal do, but I'd have thought they could stretch to a coat of paint and a call to the local glazier.

Another thing I miss from England are the players' lounges where you can relax and have a drink with your team-mates and opponents after a game. They're commonplace in England and I love a beer with the opposition, but it doesn't happen in Scotland and after the match, once the away side is changed, they go home.

The crowds in Scotland are generally much noisier than they are in England and often create a wonderful carnival atmosphere. The Rangers fans took to me very quickly and I appreciated that. When the crowd is behind you at Ibrox it's like having an extra man on the pitch and I've seen several opponents intimidated by the atmosphere the fans have created.

The game in Scotland is much faster than English football. North of the border opponents rarely run with the ball, preferring to hit long passes directly into the danger area. Purists often criticize this style, and it's not the way we like to play at Rangers, but it does provide plenty of goal-mouth action.

Consequently the game is more physical in Scotland and you have to be on your guard against high flying elbows. It can be very naughty at times and some players can get away with dodgy tackles, using their experience to talk their way out of it afterwards. There aren't really any madmen about, but the game is physical and players are aggressive and want to square up to you all the time. It's an attitude Souness is eager to get rid of at Rangers. He would prefer to harness the aggression in different ways, such as winning fifty-fifty tackles, rather than players directing it towards shaping up for a fight and appearing macho.

There is also plenty of humour in the game and the on-field banter can be very funny, with players like Dundee United's Paul Sturrock always ready to have a laugh. A couple of players have tried to provoke the Englishmen in the Rangers team, saying things like: 'You're a waste of money you lot,' and 'Who do you think you are? You're nothing.' It doesn't affect me, but Graham Roberts is guaranteed to have a go back. Opponents seem to think that Robbo will lose his head and they often niggle away at him. What they don't realize is that Robbo is always like that. When he mouths off, it's not because he's losing his cool. It's part of his normal game.

Graham Roberts was brought up in the Steve Perryman and Paul Miller school of back-chat and seems to have been a good pupil. In training games he's just the same and some of the things he comes out with are hilarious.

One of the highlights of training is the regular five-a-side between England and Scotland. If we're short we adopt Ally McCoist as an honorary Sassenach because he used to play for Sunderland reserves. The games are always keenly contested and the winners carp on about the result for the rest of the week.

The English lads settled in well. Rita and I found a marvellous house in Bridge of Allan and Chris and Sarah Woods live just down the road in Dunblane. It's a beautiful part of the country and from our kitchen window we have a fantastic view towards Stirling Castle. I know of so many players who have been unhappy after moving to a new club but Rita and I have no complaints. We've made friends in the town and even our local GP, Ian Cathcart, is a referee in the Scottish League. In fact, Bridge of Allan had a stake in all three major Scottish competitions in my first season north of the border. I won medals in the League and League Cup and the Scottish Cup was won by St Mirren, whose manager, Alex Smith, also lives in the town.

Another big reason for my decision to go to Scotland was the prospect of playing in Europe. With English clubs still banned following the Heysel disaster, it was a carrot which Graeme Souness dangled successfully before me. I'd loved the big European games when I was with Ipswich and, of course, I had fond memories of winning the UEFA Cup in 1981. You can't beat a good European match and with the floodlights on and a big crowd, there's always a great atmosphere.

Our first UEFA Cup game was against the Finnish side Ilves Tampere with the first leg at Ibrox. They started off with some brutal tackling, hoping to try and hassle us out of our game. But Davie Cooper and Ted McMinn ran rings round the Finnish defence that night and we won 4–0. Ted had one run where he beat three or four defenders to get to the byline, looked up to see who was in the middle waiting for the cross, swung his left foot at the ball and missed it completely. He ended up in a tangled heap on the floor as the ball rolled off harmlessly for a goal-kick, but the crowd loved it and gave him a tremendous cheer. The Scottish fans love a character and Ted fits the bill perfectly.

When I first saw Ted McMinn in training I thought he was a centre-half and couldn't believe it when they said he was winger. He looked so gangly and awkward and didn't have the right stature for a forward. I first saw him play when he came on as a substitute against Tottenham in a pre-season friendly. The lads used to call him 'Tomato Face' and I soon saw why. After a couple of gangly runs his face was bright red. To the fans Ted was always 'Tin Man' but to the players he was known as 'Tomato Cooping' because he was so red in the face.

Ted's one of the most deceptive players I've ever seen. He never appears to be in control of the ball and always looks as though he's overrun it, but then he'll stretch out a leg to drag the ball back or poke it forward and defenders can't win it off him. He's so effective when he runs at the defence with his unorthodox and unpredictable style that he causes all kinds of panic and creates a number of chances. I was sad to see him go to Seville and the training ground, in particular, has been a quieter place without him.

We lost the second leg in Finland 2–0 in front of a sparse crowd of little more than 2,000. It was a poor game and we knew we had to play better than that if we were going to progress in Europe.

In the second round we were paired with Boavista of Portugal, winning the first leg at Ibrox 2–1 after being a goal down. The game was played three days before the Skol Cup final and once again Ted McMinn contrived to baffle European opposition. He came on as substitute and with his first touch he back-heeled the ball between the legs of two Boavista defenders.

It was a slender lead to take to Portugal and by conceding a goal at Ibrox we'd given ourselves a tricky return leg, but Chris Woods was in superb form, keeping yet another clean sheet. We'd been under pressure for a spell in the second half before Davie Cooper went off on one of his runs, beating three defenders and laying the ball off for Derek Ferguson. His shot flashed past the Boavista keeper for the only goal of the night, giving us a 3–1 win on aggregate. For the first time in eight seasons Rangers were through to the third round of a European competition.

Our opponents were Borussia Moenchengladbach and once again the first leg was at Ibrox. The Germans had beaten Partizan Belgrade and Feyenoord in earlier rounds, winning both of their away legs in the process, so we knew we faced a good team. Initially we were drawn away from home in the first leg, but UEFA switched the tie because Borussia's neighbours, Bayer Uerdingen, were also drawn at home that night and their tie had come out of the hat first.

Walter Smith, our assistant manager, had seen Borussia play and our preparations were helped by some Rangers fans in West Germany who sent us videotapes of Borussia matches. There's a special rivalry between the British and the Germans and this night was no exception. It was a horrible, wet evening and Borussia seemed cocky before the kick-off. But we started well and took the lead after fifteen minutes, Ally McCoist flicking the ball on for Ian Durrant to score with his left foot.

The goal put us on top and meant we were in a strong position as long as we didn't concede a goal. But that's just what we did.

Two minutes before half-time we gave the ball away in midfield. The Borussia full-back, Andrew Winkhold, broke quickly on the right and whipped in a cross for Uwe Rahn to head home, unmarked at the far post. It was a classic counter-attack goal and the kind we should never have given away, especially at that time.

In the interval the gaffer was justifiably angry, but the damage was done and a few heads had dropped. The gaffer was trying to be positive and lift us saying: 'Come on you lot, we can do it.' But in the second half we just weren't the same and when the game ended in a 1–1 draw, the Germans were delighted.

The return leg in the Bokelberg stadium was as explosive as our first League game of the season against Hibernian. The villain as far as I'm concerned was the referee, Mr Alex Ponnet of Belgium. He was inconsistent and not up to the standard of some of the British officials I've played with. We could see that he was nervous and tense and it was impossible to communicate with him. He missed the linesman's flag several times and ignored some of the brutal German tackling.

Borussia had adopted their own tactical strategy over the two games based on kicking and body-checking. It was deliberate provocation. European teams seem to think that Scottish teams will lose their heads and they laid into us. Ted McMinn received some of the worst treatment and his legs were a mass of cuts and bruises after the game, but the referee gave us no protection.

Our best chance came early on, Ally McCoist hitting the bar with a superb dipping shot. I was pulled down for a blatant penalty, but Mr Ponnet waved play on, even to the surprise of some of the German players. Inevitably frustration began to set in. Stuart Munro was sent-off for retaliation. He'd been hacked down and as he lay on the ground the man who had fouled him, continued to kick him. Stuart flicked out a boot in self-protection. Compared to the tackle, there was certainly no malice but the referee sent him off. The game exploded.

Davie Cooper went next. He'd had enough and told the referee what he thought. I don't know how I stayed on the pitch. I was so angry. It's a good job Mr Ponnet hasn't got a good grasp of English swear-words. When the final whistle went I started arguing the point with him and had to be restrained by Graeme Souness. A photographer jumped in front of me and I was about to bury his camera in his face until he started pleading in a broad Scottish accent 'No, no. I'm one of you.'

Games like that leave a bad taste in the mouth. With a stronger official we would have got a result. We were the better side over the two legs but still went out.

I think most teams prefer to play the first leg of a European tie away from home, because you then know what you have to do in the second leg in front of your own fans. But Rangers had always been at home in the first leg and that creates extra pressure. In European football, teams come to stop you playing. If I was a manager bringing a team to Ibrox, I would send my team out to frustrate Rangers and wait for the crowd to turn against them. With no rival fans to sing against, the home supporters are quieter and seem to become restless if the home side doesn't score early on.

Our UEFA Cup hopes may have gone but at least we were still in contention for the League and the Scottish Cup. Graeme Souness had made it clear from the start that the trophy he wanted more than any other was the League title. But we'd had a disappointing start and with a quarter of the season gone we were third behind Celtic who'd taken over at the top from the early leaders, Dundee United.

We slipped further behind after losing at home to Motherwell. We'd dominated the game until they scored the winner through Ray Farmingham with two minutes to go in their first attack of the match. We beat Clydebank and Dundee but then lost 1–0 at Pittodrie in a bad-tempered game which saw Dave McPherson sent off. That defeat left us eight points behind Celtic with just over half the season to go and few people gave us any chance of winning the League at that time.

But in December we started an impressive run of seven successive wins which eroded Celtic's lead and put us on top of the table for a week before we dropped a point in a disappointing scoreless draw at home to Aberdeen.

One of the main influences in this run was our newest signing, Graham Roberts, who'd cost £450,000 from Spurs.

He made his début in our 2–0 win against Dundee United and the crowd took to him immediately. He's all heart and commitment and skilful with it. In his third game he scored a remarkable goal. We were away to Motherwell on a bone hard pitch and Robbo chested down a clearance from the 'Well defence. He was just inside their half and everyone thought he was going to play the ball out to the wing. Instead he drilled a tremendous shot which flew into the top corner for the only goal of the game.

Robbo reads the game well and is much more intelligent than people give him credit for. He thinks about the game and he's got a lot of experience. He talks incessantly and his will to win rubs off on his team-mates. He's an inspirational figure and I'm sure he would make an excellent captain. He's a tremendously powerful tackler and very protective towards his team-mates.

As well as the new signings from England, the manager also introduced some pre-match routines from the Continent, including taking the players to a hotel for the night before a game. Some players were quite happy with this, but I was used to being at home and felt happier in my own bed. After a while the manager let those of us who preferred to be at home do so, while others, mainly the young, free and single, stay at a hotel where they are sure of a good night's sleep.

Footballers are often creatures of habit and I've developed my own match-day routine, which I don't like being disturbed. I always have a lie-in on a Saturday morning to get as much rest as possible. The children are banned from the bedroom, although Edward, my youngest son, always manages to sneak in and try to play some game or other. At 10.15 Rita brings me a cup of milky coffee, made in the microwave.

I rarely eat breakfast, but occasionally I'll have a croissant or a slice of toast before I get ready. I leave the house at about 11.15. I'm terrible company on Saturday mornings. My mind is so concentrated on the game that I'm hopeless to talk to. If we have visitors I stay locked away in my bedroom.

On the drive to Glasgow I usually play a couple of tapes, normally heavy metal. There's nothing like driving along the motorway with Gary Moore blaring out on the stereo. The team meet for a pre-match meal in the Grosvenor Hotel in Glasgow at around midday. I always have tea and toast. One day I changed my order and had grilled fish and we lost 1–0 to Motherwell. Since then I've stuck with toast.

After lunch most of the lads watch 'Saint and Greavsie' or 'Football Focus' where there's generally a bit of banter as the Scots and English trade friendly insults. Once the television football programmes finish there's an empty hour. It's the worst part of the day for me. My mind is on the game and I can't concentrate on anything else, but there are still two hours to kill before the kick-off.

For home games we have to be at Ibrox at 1.45 and even at that time there are always thousands of fans outside the ground. I seem to sign hundreds of autographs between the car park and the main entrance. At two o'clock the manager calls a meeting where he names the side and gives his team talk. He likes everyone to be changed and out on the pitch by half past two for a warm-up. Sometimes we'll play 'piggy in the middle' where the piggy has to intercept the ball as the rest of us pass it to each other. It's a good exercise to sharpen you up before a game.

We go back inside at 2.45 to put on our pads, vaseline our eyebrows and go through other last minute preparations. Ally McCoist is always the last person to get changed, and as kick-off approaches players go into their own routines. Davie Cooper becomes very quiet, while the gaffer looks very determined and keeps saying: 'Come on you so-and-so's. Let's go and do them.' I'm loud and as we line up to go out, I normally shout encouragement such as, 'First twenty minutes lads,' or 'Early shout sorts it out,' 'Back each other up in tackles,' and so on. They're all clichés but it's not so much what you say that's important, as making sure everyone has the right attitude. I tend to be noticed because of my height. It's important for a big beefy man to make a noise and it can also intimidate opponents. If he's quiet it gives the impression he's a wimp or easy meat.

A bell rings when it's time for us to go out. The changing rooms at Ibrox are deep underneath the main stand and when you open the door you can hear the build up of noise in the stadium. We walk along a corridor and then across a concreted warm-up area which leads to the tunnel. As you get closer to the pitch the noise of the fans gets louder and your heart starts beating faster. When you arrive at the tunnel you get your first view of the fans in the Govan Stand opposite and as soon as they see you there's a great roar which spreads round the ground.

It's a great feeling. I always run on to the pitch at full speed with my fists clenched and teeth gritted. As far as I'm concerned it's more impressive than just strolling on and it looks as though you mean business.

We often have a mascot which was a regular feature at Ipswich but quite new in Scotland. I always go through a few exercises with him which the crowd love and they always receive a big cheer. At the toss-up I always follow the motto 'Tails never fails' and it seems to work for me as I win 75 per cent. I like to kick towards the Broomloan end in the first half and the only games we lost at Ibrox in my first season were when we kicked the other way.

One thing I noticed in Scotland was the way teams always run off at half-time and at the final whistle. It doesn't happen in England and the Rangers lads say it's normally so cold on the pitch, they run to get into the warm. I'm usually too tired to run and after forty-five minutes I can't wait for two cups of tea, hot and sweet just the way I like it. Some of the lads have orange or a vitamin drink to replace the energy we've lost on the pitch.

The gaffer makes everyone sit down and then goes through his comments on the first half. 'Right, you bastards,' he says or sometimes stronger if we're not playing well. Then Walter Smith makes a few points before it's open for anyone else to make any comments. The lads appreciate that. Nobody likes a dictator running the team and it's good for the management to have feedback from the players.

I don't like sitting down for too long during the break and I'm always on the move. Doddy, the kit-man, brings round a clean set of shirts for those who want them. I never bother, but some, like the gaffer, will change everything except their socks. Then when the referee's ready he puts his head round the door and calls us out for the second half.

At full-time we always have the television on in the changing rooms to watch the other results come in on the 'Grandstand' teleprinter. I always look out for Ipswich's result and take a lot of stick if they lose. I like to wind down after a game with a couple of cups of tea and then have a long bath or shower. Often a couple of newspaper reporters wait outside for a few words about the game and most weeks the players are encouraged to do some PR work for the club by having a drink in the executive lounge with some of the supporters.

It's a routine that I follow every Saturday. It's comfortable and helps me prepare mentally for the game. I'd gone through the same routine on the morning of our Third Round Scottish Cup at home to Hamilton at the end of January 1987.

We'd played Hamilton in the League ten days earlier and won 2–0, although Graham Roberts and Ian Durrant were both sent off. That win had put us on top of the Premier Division while Hamilton were firmly rooted to the bottom with only three wins so far that season. Rangers had never lost to Hamilton in the Scottish Cup so all the omens pointed to a victory for us. But as my manager at Ipswich, Bobby Ferguson, was fond of saying, football has a nasty habit of kicking you in the teeth.

When I drove into Glasgow on the morning of the game I felt on a high. Everything was going well, we'd put a good run together and were challenging for the League, the England international team was going well, it was the New Year and everything seemed rosy. It was a lovely sunny day and I was looking forward to another good cup run, feeling the contentment that comes when you're on top of your job. I was totally unprepared for the nightmare that followed.

I didn't think we played too badly and we created more than a dozen chances but couldn't score. Hamilton had come to defend and their goalkeeper, Davie McKellar, had a marvellous game. They hadn't mounted an attack until twenty minutes from the end when they pumped a long ball forward, Dave McPherson miscontrolled it and Adrian Sprott, the Hamilton left-back, burst through to score.

It was the first goal we'd conceded in thirteen games. We kept pressing but the goal wouldn't come and we were out of the Scottish Cup. A lot was made of the fact that it was twenty

years that month since Rangers had lost to Second Division
Berwick Rangers in the First Round of the Scottish Cup. That
had been one of the biggest shocks in Scottish football and
people started talking about the Hamilton result in the same
light. We've had opposition fans taunting us with chants of
'Hamilton' for the rest of the season. Results had been going
so well for us that none of the players had envisaged losing.
Chris Woods, Dave McPherson and I had arranged to go out
with our wives that evening to celebrate the start of our cup
run and not surprisingly it wasn't the jolly occasion we'd
planned.

All good sides will lose at some time, but it's how they react
to a defeat that reveals how good they are. We had to be
positive and concentrate on the League. We bounced back the
following week with a 5–2 win at Hearts – the first time they'd
been beaten at Tynecastle for more than eighteen months. It
was a comprehensive victory and exactly the result we needed.
Ironically, twenty years earlier, the Rangers team that had lost
to Berwick also went to Tynecastle the following week. They
too beat Hearts and then went on to win the League. It was a
good omen for us.

The following week Ally McCoist scored a hat-trick in our
3–1 win at St Mirren. The championship race was hotting up
and seven days later we were back on top. We only drew 1–1
at home to Hibs, but Celtic lost 4–1 at Dundee. We had the
same points but our goal difference was better and we also had
a game in hand.

As the run-in started we won five games in succession in
March and built up a four-point lead over Celtic. At the beginning of April we faced the Old Enemy at Parkhead with nearly
61,000 fans packed into the ground. The atmosphere was
incredible. Celtic were fired up and were awarded two penalties
in three minutes towards the end of the first half. Brian McClair
scored both times and, although Ally McCoist pulled one back
for us, Owen Archdeacon scored a third for Celtic to wrap up
the game. It opened up the title race again, although the
championship would definitely be ours if we took maximum
points from our last five games.

Although it wasn't well known at the time, I was struggling
with a pelvic injury. It left me in agony after each game and I

was in pain every time I walked. I was unable to train between matches and the doctors told me that the only cure was rest.

By now the tension was getting to the fans and the crowd seemed more nervous than the players when we met Dundee in a re-arranged midweek game at Ibrox. Goals from Davie Cooper and Ally McCoist gave us a 2–0 win and helped us to relax. On the Saturday we beat Clydebank 3–0, while Celtic dropped a point at home to Dundee United, conceding the equalizer in the last minutes of the game.

We beat Hearts 3–0 and went to Aberdeen knowing that a draw would be enough to bring the championship back to Ibrox for the first time in nine years.

Once again it was an explosive match. After half-an-hour we were down to ten men when Graeme Souness was sent off for the second time that season.

Minutes later we took the lead. Davie Cooper floated in a free-kick and I launched myself at the ball and got a good header. I thought the ball was going wide but it seemed to swerve in at the last minute. It was only my second goal of the season but I couldn't have timed it better in terms of value to the team. By half-time Aberdeen were level, Irvine scrambling the ball home after we failed to clear a corner.

Rangers had warned fans not to travel unless they had tickets for the game. The official allocation was 5,000, but there were at least twice as many Rangers fans inside Pittodrie and about 10,000 outside the ground. I'd never known supporters like it. They roared us on through the second half and, although Aberdeen hit the post, we never felt like losing. With about five minutes to go a tremendous cheer went round the ground. We knew that Celtic had been drawing at home to Falkirk but couldn't work out what the cheer was for until one of the fans behind the goal told Jimmy Nicholl that Falkirk had taken the lead. It meant the title was almost certainly ours. The fans were going crazy and when the final whistle went they invaded the pitch in their thousands. Somehow the Aberdeen players got back to the changing rooms but we were swamped. Ally McCoist lost a gold chain in the mêlée and had both his boots pinched by souvenir hunters. A group lifted me on to their shoulders and tried to carry me round the pitch.

It was pandemonium. The police eventually forced a passage

through the crowd for us to get back to the changing rooms but there was no way they could disperse the fans. The 10,000 fans who'd been outside the ground for the game had found a way to join in the celebration.

Memories of that Aberdeen game will live with me for the rest of my life. I'd waited a long time to be a champion and now I'd achieved it. I eventually fought my way into the dressing room after a couple of policemen forced their way through the crowd to help me to safety. We could hear the fans singing outside while inside there was beer flying everywhere as the celebrations began. There was a tremendous feeling of relief as if in one magic moment all the pressures of the season had been lifted. The lads were in full song, but the most moving sight for me was Ian Durrant who was sitting with his head in hands and crying his eyes out. He was only twenty and to win the League, especially with the team that he'd always supported, was an incredible feat.

Aberdeen supplied us with beer and, although a few lads changed and jumped into the bath, I was happy to sit there in my dirty kit savouring the moment. We could hear the Rangers fans in full voice and then Alastair Hood, the club's Operations Officer, put his head round the door and said: 'The fans want you to do a lap of honour.'

We didn't need any persuading and those of us who weren't in the bath were back out on to the Pittodrie pitch to share our success with the fans. The celebrations continued on the way home. We stopped at a hotel to buy a case of champagne and five crates of lager. Drink is banned on coaches, but on that occasion we were prepared to suffer the consequences. There was one dodgy moment when we reached Forfar and came up against a diversion. The manager spotted a line of policemen directing the traffic and shouted out: 'Hide the booze lads, put your glasses down.' Our coach had 'Rangers FC' on the front and luckily the police on duty were all Rangers fans. Instead of booking us for drinking they gave us a big cheer and waved us on our way. It was an incredible journey. We passed thousands of Rangers supporters who'd lined the route and there were even farmers in their fields giving us the thumbs up as we drove past.

The coach dropped Chris Woods, Dave McPherson and

myself in Dunblane and we had some more champagne at Woodsy's house before going off for a meal and then ending up in a night-club in Stirling with Stuart Munro and his wife. It was a marvellous evening and even Celtic supporters were coming up and offering to buy us drinks.

I was delighted that our season had ended so well after such an inauspicious start. The team had taken time to come good but had stuck together through thick and thin and that team spirit was partly responsible for our success. The supporters had been magnificent all season. They could have turned on us early on when we lost two of our first three games, but they remained firmly behind us and we were able to reward them with two trophies.

Winning the Skol Cup so early was an important shot in the arm but one of the key factors in our League success was the signing of Graham Roberts. He arrived at just the right time and was the perfect new face whose commitment to Rangers matched that of even the most loyal fan. He blended into the team immediately and we struck up an understanding straight away.

The gaffer adopted a 4–4–2 system with Ally McCoist and Robert Fleck up front, although occasionally he dropped Flecky to accommodate a five-man midfield with just Ally up front. We used this system in Europe and against Celtic in the Skol Cup final and they found it hard to combat. But above all, the main reason for our success was the manager himself. He's always been the type of player you'd rather have on your side than playing against you and I wish I could have teamed up with him earlier in my career. He's been the driving force all season and it was his influence and will to win that spurred us to success.

My season wasn't over yet. After our final League game, at home to St Mirren where we were presented with the League Championship trophy, the Rangers team flew to Israel for an end-of-season tour. Then I came back to play for England against Brazil at Wembley in an exciting 1–1 draw. Fittingly, my final game of the season was at Hampden Park in the annual fixture between Scotland and England. I had been looking forward to the game all year and for the first time the England side contained more Rangers players than the

Scotland team, with both myself and Chris Woods in the line-up. I was marking Ally McCoist, my Rangers team-mate. Unfortunately the game was disappointing, ending in a 0–0 draw.

There's such a high profile build-up towards this fixture that it seems wrong to play it at the end of a long hard season when players on both sides are exhausted. It's the oldest international fixture in the world and still interests fans and players both sides of the border. But the game is in danger of becoming nothing more than an exhibition match. If we're to keep interest alive, the game should be played earlier in the season when the players are still fresh. Then we'll give the fans something to shout about once more.

16

The Future

Football has been in the doldrums for too long but there are signs that the game is starting to pick itself up. Clubs have started to play more attacking football and crowds are up, especially in Scotland. But although the signs for the future may seem encouraging I believe that widespread changes are needed to make sure the game continues to flourish.

It's vital for everyone who earns their living from football that we keep the fans coming through the turnstiles. Clubs have to make greater efforts to attract customers and should do everything they can to make grounds safe for people to watch a game. We need to see more families coming to matches. The sport can't afford to lose the youngsters who are football's future. Some clubs have set up family enclosures, but these are often tucked away in obscure and sometimes windswept and unsheltered corners of the ground when they should be comfortable and welcoming.

In Scotland the grounds are often in a poor condition and in desperate need of modernization. In England most of the top clubs have spent money improving their grounds, building new stands and providing better facilities for the supporters. For example, Ipswich's ground is one of the best in the country and teams like Spurs and Manchester United have brought their stadiums up to date.

Executive boxes bring in valuable extra revenue for clubs and I'm sure Scottish teams will follow English clubs in introducing them, but clubs mustn't forget the loyal fans who turn out in all weathers. We can't take their custom for granted. We must remember that admission prices are high – perhaps too high. If there are two or three home games in a fortnight it's too expensive for the average family man to come to each one, especially if he likes to bring his children. I would like to see special rates and package deals for fans. Many supporters are unemployed or in low paid jobs. We mustn't exclude them by charging too much to see a game of football.

Hearts have shown the way forward by encouraging their fans to become more involved with the club. The supporters are invited to come and have a drink and a chat with the players after the game which is a good idea. The fans put a lot into the club and some spend a fortune following their favourite team. They deserve something in return.

Hearts have set up a junior club for supporters between the ages of five and fourteen which has attracted between 4,000 and 5,000 members and represents a promising future for the club. Hearts also offer low-cost travel to away games, providing up to forty coaches for some matches and they regularly take between 5,000 and 10,000 supporters with them.

The directors, led by the chairman, Wallace Mercer, have gone out of their way to make the supporters feel part of the club. Hearts were one of the first clubs in Scotland to introduce video cameras to monitor crowds and having identified people who were likely trouble-makers they invited them along to the club to find out why they behaved in the way they did. It made the trouble-makers aware that they could be seen, so their behaviour improved, but the club's efforts to understand and solve a problem also made them feel that they were part of the Hearts set-up.

Branches of the supporters' club hold shares in Hearts and representatives from Tynecastle regularly attend supporters' club meetings in an effort to keep open the lines of communication between the fans and the Hearts officials. The club has also started a continuous programme of ground improvements.

Such forward thinking has paid off. Since the early 1980s gates at Tynecastle have risen from an average 4,000–5,000 each week to regular gates of 16,000 plus. And they have created a carnival atmosphere, especially when they travel.

Quite a few fans go in fancy dress and at Ibrox we saw a Father Christmas and a Pink Elephant behind the goal. Apparently the craze started when a pub in Edinburgh offered free travel to away games for any fans who came in fancy dress and it's caught on ever since.

I'm opposed to what seems to be a slow shift towards artificial pitches. As far as I am concerned football should be played on grass and plastic pitches should be banned. I loathe them. They are horrible to play on and I've never enjoyed a game on plastic. The ball runs on and on, the bounce is different, there's no give and it's harder to tackle. I share other players concern about injuries and I'm convinced that plastic pitches can cause long term harm to players' joints. The sooner they are ploughed up the better and unless they are scrapped they will kill football.

I am also opposed to those people who want to fiddle about with the rules. Getting rid of the off-side rule, for example, is not going to bring millions of people back into football grounds. It can be frustrating, but it's up to players to find a way to break it down. Teams that play the off-side trap know it can be dangerous and a fast player breaking from deep can cause them problems.

Others have suggested changing the rules so that off-side only applies in the area of the pitch eighteen yards from goal. Again I don't see this as an improvement and I believe it would make the game a duller spectacle. The play would be stretched out from penalty-area to penalty-area. Inevitably it would become slower and there would be no exciting runs from players like Gary Lineker and no space for incisive, defence-splitting passes from players like Glenn Hoddle.

The introduction of three points for a win in the English Football League in 1981 seems to have been popular with the fans who've been able to see their team leap several places up the table following a run of three or four wins. But it can be a nightmare for players. I prefer the old fashioned two points for a win and one for a draw, which is still in use in Scotland. There's more at stake with the three points system and teams which go a goal up are even more likely to sit back and hold on for victory than they would in the old system. It also puts players on a knife-edge and leads to inconsistent performances. There are some other strange systems in operation around the world. In Bulgaria, neither side gets a point if the game ends 0–0 and in Russia teams only pick up points from their first ten drawn games. Any draws after that and they come away with nothing. It would take a brave man to introduce such radical moves to the game here.

One change which I think is inevitable is the introduction of a British Superleague, with the top teams from England, Scotland and perhaps Ireland and maybe even Wales if one of their sides can get back into the higher divisions. There were hints of such a league being formed when I signed for Rangers and the competition would have tremendous appeal with mouth-watering fixtures like Celtic v Liverpool and Rangers v Spurs.

I'm sure the day will come when there will be a European League which would be very exciting. I would like to see one introduced before the end of my career, but I feel it may take longer. Supporters have shown their appetite for big European matches and I would love to see the cream of the British clubs in competition with top European opposition each week.

I don't think it would harm domestic football in England or Scotland. With our top teams playing in the European League the home championships would be more open. In Scotland teams like Dundee, Hibs and Clydebank would have a greater chance of success in the Premier Division and consequently would be able to attract more financial backing. If the European League was played in midweek it could live happily alongside the traditional game at weekends.

It could also help reduce the ridiculous number of games our top players play each year. There is too much strain on the present-day footballer. He has to play too many games in a season. An international with a good team involved in a couple of cup competitions will be playing two games a week for nine months. It's inevitable that players will pick up injuries. But as soon as a player struggles because of a knock the club finds someone to replace him and he loses his place in the team.

Often players can't afford to drop out, even though they are injured, for fear of not being able to regain their place in the team. At other times they are forced to play when they know they should be resting. They can't win. If they don't play because they're not fit managers will call them cowards. If they play then they can't perform to their full ability because they are restricted by their injury. The manager decides he needs a replacement and buys another player anyway.

Injured players are often given cortisone injections to ease the pain and enable them to play. That may work for ninety minutes but in the long term the injury doesn't heal and many players have ended up cripples through playing when they should have been resting and waiting for an injury to heal.

I also disagree with people who say that footballers are over-paid. One or two players may give slight credibility to that argument through their behaviour off the pitch, but in my view footballers are under-paid. Our efforts and skills generate large incomes for our clubs and we deserve a fair share. It's a short career – there aren't many professions where you are forced to retire by the time you are thirty-five and many foot-ballers are virtually crippled by the time they are forty or fifty.

There are only a few who earn the so called big money and by comparison to other sportsmen, footballers receive modest rewards. We have no security and are open to attack by everyone. You're ridiculed in front of your family and friends when you go out and called every name under the sun from the terraces.

Your entire lifestyle is controlled by your job. You can't go out when other people are having a good time. For example, Friday night is the big night of the week for most people but we have to stay in and rest. Much of our time is spent travelling, preparing for games and you're away from your family for long periods. Football takes first place and families come second. We get paid well but we sacrifice a lot to earn our money.

Having said that, football has been good to me. I've made a good living; I live in a marvellous house; I've travelled the world; and I've been privileged to go to places I would never have dreamed of as a youngster. If it all ended tomorrow I would be able to say that football had given me a great life and when I look around some of the country's depressed areas with high unemployment, poverty and bad housing, I realize how fortunate I have been.

It annoys me to see former professionals, who have no connection with the present game, writing newspaper columns or wheeled on to television programmes because they're likely to say something controversial or outrageous. Viewers aren't idiots and they deserve better than some old 'has been' ranting away hysterically because he's being paid to be controversial. Anyone can get up and say things like: 'The manager's rubbish and should be sacked', but pandering to bigotry doesn't really add anything to people's understanding of the game. I find it sad that former players are prepared to squander opportunities to talk intelligently about football, preferring to act stupid. There are plenty of respected footballers who can be informative and entertaining and would make far better television panellists than the loudmouths.

I think television contributed to the drop in attendance at football matches. For a while you could see recorded highlights of seven or eight games a weekend and people stopped going to matches. Some say TV acted as an appetizer, but if people are undecided on whether to go to a game and they know it's going to be on the box, there's a good chance they'll stay at home and watch the highlights in the evening.

Football has much to look forward to. Rangers' success in 1986–87 prompted many fans to draw comparisons with some of the great Ibrox sides of the past. I've been compared to players like George Young and Davie Meiklejohn which was very flattering, but I think we'd developed a style of our own. The future for Rangers is very rosy. The club has a progressive board that wants success and is prepared to spend money to buy players to achieve it. Everyone connected with the club was delighted when we won the League and Skol Cup in my first season. We set a high standard and the next target is the treble. I believe Rangers will go on to become the best team in Britain.

Much has been made of the religious traditions associated with football in Scotland and it's hard for people in England to understand the strength of feeling there is north of the border. Rangers have always been Protestant and Celtic have been the Catholic club, with intense rivalry between the respective fans. At one time rumours were rife in Glasgow that I was a Catholic. Celtic fans kept coming up and congratulating me, but the truth is that I am not a Catholic. I don't think Graeme Souness bothered about my religion when he signed me and I'm sure the day will come when Rangers do sign Catholic players. As far as I am concerned religion is completely separate from football and I'm sure that the religious barrier will eventually be smashed.

As far as my future is concerned I'm under contract to play for Rangers until I'm thirty and I've every intention of honouring that. I want to see the club become the best in Europe. I couldn't have joined at a more exciting time and it's been a great thrill to be part of the spectacular revival which happened during my first season.

When my playing career is over I'll have to think hard about which direction I want to take. I had always wanted to play in a heavy metal band, but that seems unlikely now! My hair is too short to start with. I tried growing it long when I was at Ipswich but it kept getting in my eyes and I couldn't see, so Bobby Robson told me to have it cut. And there's the further problem that I can't sing or play guitar.

I have an insurance business which I set up in Ipswich in 1985 and I am obviously keen for that to succeed. But I was talking to Bryan Robson, who's six months older than I am, and we both realized that football is all we know. And having played at top level and having mixed with, listened to and learnt from some of the best in the business, I would like to think that I've picked up a few tips and I would like to put something back into the game.

I would love the chance to go into management and maybe try my hand as a player-manager while I've still got some strength in my legs. At one time my ambition was to return to Anfield as the manager of Ipswich and come away with a victory. I would still like that to happen one day. I'm aware of the pitfalls of being a football manager, the insecurity and the amount of time it eats up and takes you away from your family, but I think I would always regret it if I never gave it a try. Whether I would be hard enough after being one of the lads for so long is another question, but I'd love to have a go.

I've come a long way from the awkward, shy teenager who first arrived for a trial at Portman Road, and I'm sure that I have a long way to go. I've learnt that football, like life, is full of surprises, but to me it's still the greatest game in the world. Long may it remain so.